> To my dear frien[d] Morianna (Make a lame ... Spell your name Died as it should!) Love you, kiddo. Happy trails,

Pun and Grimeish Mint

The Lowest Form of Humor in the Highest Number of Words

Lloyd Farley

◆ FriesenPress

Suite 300 - 990 Fort St
Victoria, BC, V8V 3K2
Canada

www.friesenpress.com

Copyright © 2020 by Lloyd Farley
First Edition — 2020

All rights reserved.

No part of this publication may be reproduced in any form, or by any means, electronic or mechanical, including photocopying, recording, or any information browsing, storage, or retrieval system, without permission in writing from FriesenPress.

ISBN
978-1-5255-8812-9 (Hardcover)
978-1-5255-8811-2 (Paperback)
978-1-5255-8813-6 (eBook)

1. HUMOR, PUNS & WORD PLAY

Distributed to the trade by The Ingram Book Company

"I didn't even have to Force myself through it."
—Darth Vader

"I couldn't let it go."
—Elsa

"I laughed my head off."
—Anne Boleyn

"Me too!"
—Marie Antoinette

"Up and away the most entertaining book I've ever read"
—Superman

"Surely this is one of the greatest books of all time. And don't call me Shirley."
—Dr. Rumack

"Its made from people! Pun And Grimeish Mint is made from people!"
—Charlton Heston

"You're gonna need a bigger boat."
—Chief Brody... like, what?

Hey howdy hey, all!

The question I'm often asked is, "How do you think of these things?" Well, I dunno. I guess I don't think like normal people. It could be my passion for wordplay. It could be my desire to make people smile. It could be my quick... wit. It is more likely to be my ADHD intro/extroverted OCD maniacal Peter Pan syndromic (plus various other minor psychological maladies) nature. But who the heck knows.

Nevertheless, these puns are my gift to you. I hope they bring you joy, I hope they make you happy, I hope they make you groan, roll your eyes back in your head and pray to the first available deity to make the madness stop.

To my friends, my family, my fans. To Mumsey and Homer. To my sweet Brute and my "best friends in the galaxy," the C and C Farley Factory. To the big guy upstairs. To the things and people who contributed to my insanity – "Weird Al", Clint, Freddy, ALF, the Brady Bunch, Bruce, Monty Python, Fawlty Towers, ZAZ, Leslie, Killer Tomatoes, Plan 9, Ed, Fozzie, "I'm The Man", a van named Clarise and a narwhal named Noddy. My love and deepest thanks.

Happy trails,
Lloyd

Pictures of my wonderful children – aren't they...

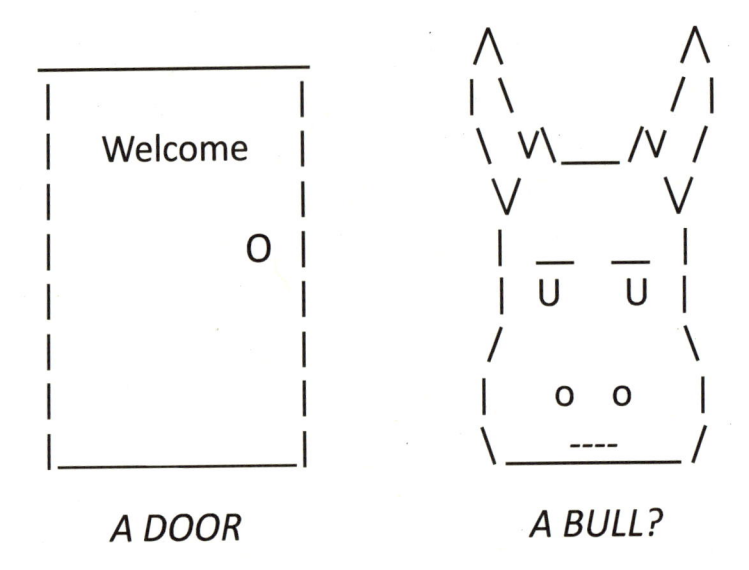

```
 _____              ^           ^
|              |             |\         /|
|   Welcome    |             | \       / |
|              |              \ v\___/v /
|          o   |               v         v
|              |              |  _   _  |
|              |              | U   U |
|              |             /         \
|              |            |   o   o   |
|_____|             _____/
                                ----
    A DOOR                      A BULL?
```

... and it goes downhill from here...

BRAINS... BRAINS...

Professor Langdon was a kindly man, yet inept at social conventions. While he could mesmerize with tale after tale of scientific breakthroughs that he or his companions had engineered, the professor was virtually unable to find or give appropriate gifts. Every birthday, every Christmas, he would stress for hours on what to give the significant people in his life yet would fail miserably every time. One day, though, he made a discovery while walking through the medical lab that changed this crippling defect in his character. "Brains!" he shouted, "I can give away pickled brains!" And so he did; for every social occasion, he found the perfect brain to give away. Nieces, nephews, parents, even his fiancee would giggle with glee over unwrapping a perfectly chosen brain. Some people may have found him crazy for doing so, but I, for one, found that it showed great presents of mind.

LUNCH NOW BOARDING

"I've done it!" Bob exploded in the thrill of the moment. "What is it, Bob?" George asked. "Only the greatest breakthrough in the world of flight engineering since the Wright brothers!" Bob replied, "Here, take a look!" George came over to Bob's desk, looked down, and almost immediately was overcome by the sheer majesty of Bob's vision. After years of ridicule from the other flight engineers, Bob had finally created the basis for a fleet of edible aircraft. No longer would aging, hulking jets be left to rust in acres of abandoned runways, but instead, they could be eaten by those in desperate need of nourishment. "Bob, this is amazing!" George said to his friend, "I never thought it could be done, but you have done it – to think, edible aircraft! What flavors would they come in?" "Well," Bob replied, "right now they would only be available in plane."

HAVE YOU SEEN YOUR SPICES, BABY, STANDING IN THE SHADOWS?

Ruby was utterly flustered. While her home wasn't small by any means, each nook, cranny, hole, and shelf in the kitchen was full. Even this wouldn't have been an issue for Ruby if her complete set of Rolling Stones' spices hadn't just arrived. She searched and searched yet could not find one square inch in which to put the latest additions to her culinary collection. Just as she was about to give up hope, inspiration struck! There, in the backyard, was her childhood playground set. "Wonderful!" she thought to herself, "I can use that playground as a spice rack!" And so she did, placing the entire set of spices in and around her playground. Later that week, her mother came to visit. As was usually the case, the two worked together on preparing a meal for the extended family. "Ruby, dear," her mother asked, "Where might the paprika be?" "Oh, that's out on my monkey bars," Ruby replied. "Salt and pepper?" "Those would be on my swings." "Cumin?" "That's on my bridge." "What about thyme, Ruby?" her mum inquired, "I just need to add some to the roast beef." "Thyme?" Ruby answered, "Thyme is on my slide."

THE LOVE OF BUGS IS...

Scientists recently discovered something absolutely fascinating about the migratory paths of beetles. Years ago, large numbers of beetles from around the globe were fitted with little mini-transmitters, and their movements tracked. While occasionally one of these beetles would meet the bottom side of a shoe, for the most part the transmitters were left intact. What the scientists discovered after studying their patterns is no matter where in the world the beetles were, they all at some point in their life's journey traversed a 10 km stretch of path in South America. While they have no understanding of why this occurs, they have marked this stretch as the route of all weevil.

I'VE LOST MY FLIPPERS

Henry looked around his majestic room, only to pause mournfully at his giant aquarium. Usually, he would see his beloved dolphin, Dolph, playing in the aquarium for hours on end, but that all changed last Tuesday. That was the day that tragedy struck – Dolph was nowhere to be found. Henry looked everywhere – under rocks, cushions, even posting pictures begging for information but to no avail. Finally, he had decided it was enough. "I can't keep looking for Dolph," he whispered to himself. "He's gone. And now, my life has no porpoise."

I'M LOOKING OVER A FOUR LEAF... WHAAAA?

Darby O'Shea waited in line at Blarney Castle in Ireland for what seemed like an eternity. As was the annual tradition, he and his mates would gather together and kiss the infamous Blarney Stone before the start of the school year for good luck and the "gift of the gab." Of course, this tended to take a tremendous amount of time as Blarney Castle was usually inundated with tourists from around the globe at this time of year. Finally, though, it was Darby's turn. As he puckered up and planted a good smooch on the stone, he noticed something awry – instead of cold stone, it almost felt like light styrofoam on his lips. Sure enough, he reached out to touch the Blarney Stone only to break off a piece and reveal that the stone was carved out of styrofoam. "Ladies and gentlemen," Darby cried out. "We've been had! This is a sham rock!!"

NO MORNING WAKE UP?

For all the publicity the case had garnered, there was an almost eerie quietness in the courtroom. The lawyers for both the defense and the prosecution looked over their notes to prepare for the day. Standing to the side, in shackles and looking forlorn, was Bert McAphee, accused of lacing the office coffee with poison. As the judge entered the courtroom, all slowly rose. After being instructed to sit again, there was a flurry of commotion at the prosecution table. "Is there a problem?" the judge asked the lead attorney. "Well, your honor," the prosecutor replied, "It seems that a key piece of evidence against the accused, a bag full of the coffee filter and used coffee beans from the day in question, has gone missing." "In that case – Mr. McAphee, you are free to go," the judge bellowed, "there are no grounds for a conviction."

TV OR NOT TV

Beatrice was absolutely repulsed by what she was seeing on the local public television station. She usually enjoyed settling in for an evening of comforting television before proceeding to bed, whether it was the Boston Pops orchestra or the latest period piece from the BBC. Tonight, though, was too much. There in full view was the televised orchestra of the evening, and while she could make out a French horn or two, and a trombone, the vision of a multitude of fiddles and saxophones was appalling. "Bah," she grunted as she turned off the TV and threw the remote to the floor, "nothing but sax and violins on TV these days."

A 14, A 7 AND AN ORDER OF RICE TO GO

The premise of the park was intriguing – one price admission for "All You Can Eat" Chinese food and access to the multi-level, expansive playground around the back. And it delivered. The food was fantastic, and the playground equipment had something for everyone, from the tame baby swing set to a five-story tall, twisty turny playground slide for the adventurous. The only thing that wasn't made clear was if you could bring the food with you to the park. "Excuse me," I gently asked one of the staff members, "I'm really enjoying this Chinese food, especially out of this Asian bowl, but was hoping I can go into the park with it." "Of course!" the young man replied, "Please, help yourself! You can take a wok on the swings, and you can take a wok on the monkey bars." He paused briefly before pointing at the 5-story slide behemoth, "You can even take a wok on the wild slide."

HAVE YOUR KAYAK AND EAT IT TOO

"C'mon, park your boat here!" they cried out, "Everyone parks here!" He tried to ignore them, but it was difficult to do so. It was a great spot to moor his boat – close to home, close to the beach, well lit. There was even a gas station on the dock that he could use to fill up. But he remembered the words his mother said all those years ago – "Just because everyone else is doing it doesn't mean you need to." These words had fared well for him over the years, and he was determined to make his own decisions on what to do. "Sorry, guys," he replied to their calls, "I'll find my own spot. I refuse to bow to pier pressure."

THIS ONE BITES

The bloodlust was almost all-consuming, and he could barely take any more. Over the years, Vlad tried everything to get over his vampirism but to no avail. As he walked through downtown Transylvania, he saw a sign over a medical clinic that read, "Cure Your Vampirism!" "Could it be true?" Vlad wondered. His heart beat faster at the thought of finally, perhaps finally, being returned to a normal life. But doubt started to creep in – Vlad really had exhausted all of the so-called cures over his life, and the search for a cure also depleted what was left of the family fortune, so why would this one be different, and could he even afford it if it was? Yet, he couldn't take it anymore, so in he went. After waiting a few minutes, the doctor came in, assessed his situation, and injected Vlad with a serum. Another few minutes later and sure enough, the bloodlust was gone, his fangs reverted to normal, and his waxy complexion glowed with a healthy rose that he hadn't seen in a millennium. "Oh, thank you, doctor!" Vlad cried out, "I am so deeply appreciative. I can't afford much, but what do I owe you?" "No worries, young man," the doctor replied, "for you, necks to nothing."

VOLLEY VOLLEY VOLLEY GET YOUR ADVERBS HERE

"Let's play!" the kids screamed. George, the camp counselor, had to think fast. Already the day had been filled with games – Red Rover, Tag, Grounders, Simon Says – but the campers were insatiable in their desire to play, and it would be a while yet before campfire and, finally and blissfully, bedtime. So he thought and thought until he remembered a game that he used to play back in the day. "Okay, kids, gather around!" George yelled, and the kids came running. "I'm going to split you in half – alright, so this side you are mugs. On this side, you are volleyball players. The object of the game is the mugs need to catch the volleyball players." "Sounds fun," one child said, "what's it called?" "The game," George replied, "is called Cups and Lobbers."

RED, BLUE, BLUE, GREEN, ACHMED, ORANGE

Joe cautiously opened the gift. He knew what he was hoping for but didn't want to be disappointed if it wasn't that. However, as the wrapping fell off, Joe knew that what was before him was what he had wanted for ages now - a pristine video game for his Xbox, complete with plastic Arabian instruments, with the color buttons needed for compatible play. "Oh thank you, thank you!" Joe screamed, "I can play as Jamaal, as Achmed, this is awesome! I can't wait to play Qatar Hero."

SMILEY SHEEP AT MIDNIGHT

The celebration upstairs was boisterous and kept Anna awake. Finally, she couldn't take anymore and promptly went up to knock on her neighbors' door. "Oh, hey, Anna!" Caitlin giggled as she answered the door, "sorry, are we keeping you up?" "Well, yes, actually," Anna replied, "what's going on?" "Check this out," Caitlin said as she gently brought Anna over to the computer screen. On the screen was a sheep with the broadest smile Anna had ever seen, strolling casually, and a map in the corner to show where it was. "See, the sheep is coming closer!" Caitlin exclaimed, "and should be here shortly after midnight!" "So?" Anna quizzically replied. "So," Caitlin countered, "it's a happy ewe nears eve party!"

WE'RE IN FOR A VAL-HALL OF A WINTER

The exhilaration of the misdeed poured adrenalin to every pore of his body as he ran swiftly to the nearest hill. He'd been curator of the museum for years, and while always fascinated by the exhibits that would come in, this one was special. Part of the "Valhalla and Vikings" display, the wooden dinner serving plate, purportedly owned by Thor himself, was exquisite. Ever since he first laid eyes on it, all he could think of was how awesome it would be to use as a sled. He couldn't shake the feeling, and today, as the snow fell upon the landscape, he simply snapped. Opening the display, he took the serving plate and ran out the door, the distant sound of alarms ringing in his ears. And now, NOW was the time. He stood atop the snow-crested hill, surveyed the surroundings, and in a flash sat upon the plate and flew down the slope, even as the police neared him. "My God!" he thought to himself, "this is more wondrous than I dreamed! Oh, what fun it is to ride in a one Norse oaken tray!"

A QUEEN OF SOUL CHRISTMAS

The house was looking more and more festive as the day went on. Martha had dressed the Christmas tree with the numerous ornaments the family had collected over the years, bringing with them joyous memories. The cookies were cooling on the countertop, homemade snowmen were leading up the stairs, and from the fireplace hung the stockings, each one lovingly decorated by Martha. In fact, there was just one more piece that needed to be added – a wreath for the front door. Last year the wreath lost a wrestling match with the dog, so Martha needed to make a new one. She agonized over how it should look for hours – she wanted unique but welcoming. Different, but homey all the same. As she pondered, she looked out the window, scanning the yard for inspiration when her eyes rested upon the franklin bush. "Of course, the franklin bush!" she cried out, "I can use the leaves and branches to make a wreath! It'll be a wreath of franklin!!"

ON THE DANCING FLORA

The invitation lay open on the island as Bob read it over. "Come As Your Favorite Flower!" was the theme, and he didn't know what to do. Bob didn't have a favorite flower to speak of – daisies if he was pressed, but otherwise, flowers held no interest for him. Yet he had to go – the boss didn't often throw social gatherings, so when he did, it was essential to try and make it if at all possible. Finally, Bob came to a decision. He threw some red construction paper around his neck and made his way to the party. "Oh, hello Bob!" the host, decked out in sunflower garb, exclaimed as Bob came to the door, "may I ask which flower you're supposed to be?" "Well," Bob replied, "I didn't know what to do, to be honest, but I rose to this occasion."

EVERYTHING BUT THE KITCHEN STINK

Agnes waited impatiently in the vet's waiting room, her beloved skunk Melvin sitting upon her knee. Usually, Melvin would greet her in the mornings by gently licking her face, his aroma wafting through her nose. But this morning she could barely get him to move, and the smell, off-putting to most but intoxicating to Agnes, did not permeate the room as per usual. She knew something was wrong, so immediately, she raced off to the vet. Finally, Agnes was invited into the examination room where Dr. Horace Race waited for her. He took Melvin in his arms and did a series of tests to see what could be wrong. After a while, he sighed, looked at Agnes, and said, "there's no easy way to say this. Melvin is broken." Agnes fought back the tears as she replied, "wait, you mean..." "Yes," Dr. Race said, "Melvin is out of odor."

THREADBARE INTERVENTION

Jimmy walked through the door and immediately recoiled in surprise. There, sitting in a circle, were those nearest and dearest to him – his parents, his wife and kids, his friends – and one fellow Jimmy had never met before. "Please, Jimmy, sit," the stranger gently spoke, "my name is Sly Kiatrist, and we would all like to have a word with you if we may." Jimmy slunk into the open chair, unsure of what was going on. He could see tears in many eyes. "Jimmy, we are here to talk to you about your carpets and mats," Sly said as his friends and family nodded. It dawned on him then – the late nights buying Persian carpets, the collection of welcome mats and area rugs he kept in the garage, the time away from work he used to roll around Carpet Warehouse – he had hit rock bottom, and it was finally coming to a head. This was an intervention. "I knew this day would come," Jimmy muttered quietly as the tears started rolling down his face, "I'm so, so sorry. I thought I had it under control, but I don't. I have a rug addiction."

ROLL BACK GREETINGS

"Well, Carl," the store manager said, "I have to say your resume is very impressive. Your references all check out, and you've been a successful greeter at a wide variety of stores." Carl smiled – he had this one in the bag. His greeting skills were exemplary, and his dream job was to bring those skills to Walmart. "However," the manager carried on, "I'm afraid we simply can't hire you today." Carl was taken aback. "But... but... you just said I had everything you are looking for? I don't understand." "Well, Carl," the manager explained, "to be honest, while you have mostly everything you are missing one key piece. Your name isn't Matthew." And there it was. Carl felt foolish – of course, Walmart only employs welcome Matts.

TIME TO BALE OUT

Farmer Jones was frustrated. Yet again, the barn floor was littered with hay. It didn't seem to matter how many times he asked his family to clean up the floor, how many times he begged them not to play in the hay – they simply carried on. So he picked up his broom and swept up the mess as he'd done a thousand times before. "I swear I have had my fill of this!" Farmer Jones muttered to himself, "every day I'm cleaning up hay." And as he proceeded, the barn floor was looking better with every sweep, but it didn't cheer his disposition at all. Finally, he spoke aloud. "I've had it!!" he cried as he picked up the last piece of hay, "this is the final straw!"

HE SNIPS, HE SCORES

The job was menial – take the orchestra's large sheet music selection and cut patterns above all pauses. He didn't understand it, but money was money these days. So day in day out, he would pore through hundreds of music scores, look for the pause signatures, and start cutting away. He knew he could go elsewhere – he was more than qualified for several other jobs – yet somehow this job appealed to him. It really was a cut above the rest.

CARETAKER, CARE GIVETH AWAY

"And the winner is... Bruce Henderson!" The crowd went wild as Bruce made his way up to the stage yet again, this time for the "Best Puke Cleanup" award. The Custodian Awards were an annual celebration of janitors, where the best of the caretaker world were nominated in various awards – Best Puke Cleanup, Best Window Cleaning, Best Mop Style, and more. Normally the awards got spread out amongst several custodians, but this year Bruce was simply unstoppable. His cleaning skills were exemplary, his manner calm and collected, and he could lay out a gym full of chairs in record time, and the Custodian Academy noticed. Finally, up to the podium, all Bruce could do was to look out among his peers and blurt out yet another torrent of thanks. And his peers knew this was special. They gave Bruce a standing ovation for his work. He had won every award this evening, and while most gave Bruce a decent chance at winning some awards, little did they know he'd sweep all categories.

DRIP, DROP, BURN

He wasn't a pyromaniac; of that, he was pretty sure, but his compulsion to slightly burn things whenever it rained was indeed rather odd. When the sun was out, when the moon rose, even if it was somewhat overcast, he had no interest whatsoever in burning. Once that first drop of precipitation hit, though, he would rapidly pull out his lighter and find the nearest available flammable object. Not to destroy it, never to destroy it, but simply to give it some light burn marks. He needed help, and he knew it, so he called up the psychiatrist his friend had suggested. "How can I help you?" the psychiatrist asked over the phone. With a heavy sigh, he cried out, "well, I'm singeing in the rain. Just singeing in the rain."

IS THERE A CON-DUCTOR IN THE HOUSE?

"I'm exhausted," Leopold told the performing arts board, "it's becoming way too much. I can't sleep, I can't eat..." And it was true. Since the beginning of the year, Leopold had been put in charge of orchestra tryouts, hiring orchestra members, and running evening rehearsals almost every night in addition to his regular duties as the Calgary Philharmonic Orchestra conductor at each performance. "I honestly just can't take anymore!" With that, Leopold flopped back into his chair, with even the effort required to speak the words taking a noticeable effect on the man. "What do you propose?" the head of the board asked. Leopold thought for a moment and replied, "Well, I think I need to take a Strauss leave." "I see," was the reply, "fine. Four weeks of Strauss leave, and then it's Bach to work."

ALL YOU NEED IS COOL WHIP

It took a while to complete, but Ringo's dream house was finally complete. He stood in the front yard, his family by his side, marveling at just how magnificent the house was. It was far from conventional – to the best of his knowledge, no one had ever used gelatin to construct housing, and even if they had the odds they would have shaped it like a hoagie, as Ringo had, were iffy at best. The sweet cherry smell of the gelatin was a welcoming aroma, and the joy of walking on the gelatin flooring made Ringo giddy. "Alrighty kids, our new home!" he exclaimed, "from now on, we all live in this Jell-O submarine."

I'LL HAVE THE MEAT LOAF

"It wasn't me, I swear!" Chuck cried out as Phil towered over him. Phil was furious. All-day, he had been looking forward to having cheese and crackers. Phil knew his roommates well, so he took every precaution to ensure that the cheese and crackers would be there when he got home from work. He had hidden the biscuits well and put bold, yellow Post-It notes on the cheese saying, "DO NOT EAT! PROPERTY OF PHIL!!" Yet when he came home, Phil noticed that there were two enormous bites taken out of his cheese. "If it wasn't you, then who the heck did it?" Phil yelled, "Thaddeus?" "Yah, yah, it was Thaddeus!" Chuck replied, "He did it!" Phil stopped for a moment. Would Thaddeus, his other roommate, have eaten the cheese? But then he remembered one very significant fact – Thaddeus had a severe cheese allergy. "LIAR!" Phil raged, "He's allergic to cheese! So I'm sorry – two out of brie ain't Thad!"

KEEPING ABREAST OF THE SITUATION

The idea was bold, exciting… unique. Fundraising efforts for breast cancer had slowed down significantly over the year, so the foundation called for an emergency fundraising meeting to come up with ideas. Most of them were tired and old – phone solicitation, door to door fundraising, ribbons – and some were just downright odd, like the suggestion to raise money by having a 24 hour Justin Beiber-athon. But this idea… This one stood out. The foundation members looked at each other excitedly when the idea first came up. It stood to raise a lot of money for research, didn't immediately seem to have any negative connotations, and was just plain neat. The idea was to call the public out to the army barracks, where a long line of army vehicles would be ready, for those willing to donate, to be painted a bright pink. The decision was made; they were moving ahead with it. After coordination with the military, the date was set. As the time neared, the foundation prepared the barracks with everything needed – the vehicles, pink paint, brushes, balloons, a snack booth, and a large banner that read, "Tanks For The Mammaries."

SMURF'S UP

"Come over here and take a look," George Amell, professional genealogist, called out to his young apprentice, "what do you see?" The young man moved toward the microscope, took a look, and said, "well, it looks like DNA, but it's all blue?" "Correct!" George replied excitedly. For years he had taken the abuse of colleagues for his investigation into the heritage of Smurfs. He had vowed to prove not only their existence but also his hypothesis about their coloring throughout history. Finally, he came across a fossilized Smurf and extracted the DNA for testing, which is what they were looking at right now. "You see? You see?" George giggled, "Smurfs do exist! And if my calculations are right, this sample comes from the dawn of creation, proving that the Smurfs have been forever in blue genes!"

IT'S ELEMENTAL MY DEAR WATSON

The sign outside the school was welcoming – "Mother Gaia's Astrological School," it read, in bright rainbow colors and a jaunty font. Sunbeam and her husband Dragonfly walked through the front doors of the school with their five-year-old son Sandcastle in tow. Today was the first day of school and was an opportunity for parents to get acquainted with the teaching staff and the program. "Please, come and sit," Ms. Moonshadow beckoned, "Welcome to the first-grade room!" They looked around and were immediately impressed at the collection of astrological sign blocks, crystals, and other assorted New Age paraphernalia for youngsters. "Well, this is lovely!" Sunbeam exclaimed, "I see you are teaching several things here. Do you also teach the four-element alphabets?" "Indeed!" Ms. Moonshadow replied, "We teach the Earth A to G alphabet, the Fire P to T alphabet, the Air U to Z alphabet and of course the Water H to O."

IT JUST GETS VERSE FROM HERE

She was nothing if not stubborn. Her friends tried everything to get her to move into campus housing at the local university, but she would not budge. No amount of begging, pleading, or bribery was working. She had to move in soon – the school year was about to start, and the housing units were filling up quickly – but despite her friends' insistence, she had things to do first. She finally came across the old family Bible she had been searching for and flipped through it quickly until she got to her favorite passage, Psalm 23. She took her time reading it, savoring every word, and once done, she put the Bible down, entered the housing unit, and exclaimed to her friends, "Alright, I'm ready." Her friends were happy, of course, but a little perplexed as to what had happened. They shouldn't have been, though. She did always say it was the psalm before the dorm.

OUR PRICES ARE SO LOW. THEY'RE AT LEAST SIX FEET UNDER

The cast had assembled at the theatre for a read-through of Arnold's newest play, "Dead Lemons." Arnold Zifflin was the hottest playwright in town, and to be selected to star in one of his plays was an honor for any actor. So they hungrily grabbed their scripts and sat down, eager to begin the process. As they read through, they were captivated by the wordplay, enamored with the stage directions, and thrilled with the roles they were assigned. All but Tony. As Tony flipped through the pages, he began to realize that he would be on stage for the majority of the play and bore the lion's share of lines as well. He liked his character just fine, a young man that would only sell used vehicles from funeral homes, but all he could think was, "where will I find the time to re-hearse?"

MY SWOOSH HAS GONE WHOOSH

He looked out in his backyard and counted again, "One...two...three...four..." He sighed heavily – this count confirmed the sad truth. Someone had stolen a number of his basketball nets from his vast collection of basketball nets. It was an odd collection to most, but he loved it. He had basketball nets from each NBA team, nets that had been touched by the likes of Bird, Jordan, even Bryant. It was his passion, and now someone had come in and taken away pieces from his collection. Collecting himself, he quickly dialed the local police to file a report. "Yes, officer," he struggled to speak, "I am positive they have been stolen, but I don't know who would have done it. I want to believe all will turn out well, but my hoops have gone astray."

THE DEAL WITH THE O'NEAL

Henry was furious. Sure the family dogs, Barney and Betty, had on occasion chewed up things around the house, but nothing that meant so much. Until now. As he scanned the floor, all he could see was his precious NBA card collection strewn from one end of the room to the other. Some escaped damage, most were chewed up, and some... well, some were simply eaten. As he picked up the cards, he went through his mental checklist – here was his signed Dr. J card, thankfully untouched, here was his rare Larry Bird card, slightly bent but salvageable... It took a while, but he did finally get all of the cards picked up. It was then that his face went pale as he realized his most prized possession, a one-of-a-kind Shaquille O'Neal signed card, possibly worth hundreds of dollars, was missing. Collecting himself, he called over both dogs and looked sternly at them. Betty was rather calm about this, but Barney could barely look at Henry. "I see," Henry thought to himself, "Betty had nothing to do with this. She's a good pup." So he focused his attention solely on the boy pup as it became clear that the Shaq was in the male.

LADIES AND GENTLEMEN, BUOYS, AND GULLS...

The museum was strange, to say the least. Every nook, every cranny was filled with stuffed animals staged to appear as significant moments in history. There was an exhibit that envisioned the people involved in the signing of the Declaration of Independence as frogs. Another staged mice as being the first to walk on the moon. If you wanted to know what Woodstock would have looked like with llamas, you looked to your left. Shirley Johnson had worked here for years and was the lady primarily responsible for creating these taxidermied tableaus. Today she was inspired – they had never had an exhibit that showed the events of Kitty Hawk in 1903 that led to the invention of aircraft, but by golly, she was going to make one. So she had a couple of seabirds on hand that she dressed in period garb, named them Orville and Wilbur, and had them staged next to a replica of the glider used that day. When the museum opened the next day, a large sign greeted the customers that read, "Come check out our new Kitty Hawk flight exhibit!" People were excited to see it, but at first, they couldn't find where in the museum the exhibit was until Shirley indicated that they just make a couple of Wright terns.

CHRISTMAS KEE BADHAAEEYAAN, PLEASE DON'T STING ME

Aisha stared in her closet, unsure of what to wear. The company Christmas party was an exciting, fun event, and she loved going every year. This year, though, she wanted to take this opportunity to not only celebrate Christmas but to honor her Hindu heritage as well. It was a tall order to be sure, but it was important to her. So she flipped through the dozens of garments she had accumulated over the years – too red, too dark, too light… Finally, she settled on one, a lovely long cloth with yellow and black stripes, traditionally worn at Christmas. She draped the fabric around her and stormed out the door, not wanting to be late. "Oh my!" her friend Callie exclaimed as Aisha walked through the door, "that is absolutely gorgeous! What is it?" "Well, Callie," Aisha replied, "it's a Yule bee sari."

SCALPEL... SYRINGE... SNOWMAN...

The coughing kept getting worse. No matter what Sandra tried, the coughing fits plagued her night and day. It couldn't be happening at a worse time either – Christmas was just around the corner, and the whole Klaus family was coming to her house for dinner. Yet the coughing was so bad that she could barely even stand up, let alone make dinner. Finally, barely able to speak or move, she had to call 911 for an ambulance. Sandra was wheeled into Emergency and was seen by the doctor right away. "Dear God!" the doctor cried out, "get me a sterile set of tongs, stat!" As soon as the tongs were in his hands, he had the nurses hold Sandra down as he wrestled the tongs deep into Sandra's mouth. Having found what he was looking for, he pulled the tongs out rapidly, and to the great relief of all Sandra's coughing ceased right away. "Oh, doctor, I can't thank you enough!" Sandra beamed, "What on earth was happening?" He held aloft the tongs, from which a large number of silvery strands hung, and said, "You had these Christmas decorations stuck in your throat. I had to perform an emergency tinsellectomy."

MAG-NEATO

It was perplexing, indeed. No matter where Billy went, it was just a matter of time before hordes of people surrounded him. There was no safe place – people would break into his home as he slept, rap on the bathroom door if he was in there, even run after Billy's car as he would try and drive away. What was even stranger is that not one person could explain why they were hovering over Billy. The scientific community was dumbfounded as to what could be happening. There had to be a reason for it, but what could it be? One day, one of the scientists that were looking into the occurrences shouted, "Eureka! I've got it!" The other scientists ran over. "Well, what is it?" they asked. "Look at these blood samples. These are taken from the people surrounding Billy. What do you notice?" he said. One of his cohorts, looking into the microscope, said, "There is an unusually high iron content in their blood." "Exactly! Why wouldn't they be drawn towards him? Billy has such a magnetic personality."

I'VE GOTTA BEEF TO SETTLE

The function was somewhat reserved but by no means a stuffy affair. The wine flowed freely, the appetizers made the rounds, and the conversation ranged from hushed tones to uproarious laughter. Gil organized the event, and as he looked around, he was delighted with how well it was turning out. The cows were talking with the chickens. The pigs were deeply engaged in conversation with the deer. Why even the quiet bison were enjoying mingling with the turkeys. As he came to the front of the room, Gil cleared his throat, grabbed the microphone, and smiled as he said, "Hello, one and all! I'm thrilled you could all make it here tonight. Drink, eat, enjoy, and use this time as a little meat and greet."

I BEG YOUR PARDON, MA'AM-MAL

The boy was quickly getting on Adam's nerves. He had been planning this trip to the zoo with his nephew for ages, but what should have been a fun adventure was rapidly going downhill. The smaller animals were fine – the boy seemed to enjoy seeing those – but every time they approached a large mammal exhibit, he would cry out to the beasts, "You suck! You, ugly poo poo face – yah, you, you suck!!" It was not only rude but impossibly embarrassing for Adam. The final straw came as he tried to trudge away from the hippopotamus exhibit, as the boy would continue his beratement even louder, crying, "you've got a big butt! You stink!" until the poor mammals were well out of view. He pulled the boy aside and, trying to be as patient and rational as he could with his young nephew, sighed and said, "Why are you so mean to the large mammals in the zoo here?" The reply was almost instantly infuriating. "I dunno." "Well, this stops now!" Adam firmly stated, "there will be no ice cream if you can't stop being so hippo critical."

I CAN SEE CLEARLY NOW. AND THROUGH

"Congratulations, Invisible Man and Woman! You are having a baby, and so far, the child is healthy and growing!" The Invisibles were delighted! They had been trying for years to have a baby and had almost given up hope, but here was the news they had waited so long to hear. "Oh, thank you, Doc!" Invisible Man reached out his hand, "I don't know how we can thank you!" "Please, you lovely couple did all the work!" the doctor replied as he fumbled around, trying to find the Invisible Man's hand to reciprocate a hearty handshake. "What are our next steps, doctor?" the Invisible Woman asked. The doctor turned to the general direction of the voice and said, "Well, keep on a healthy diet, don't overdo anything, try not to get overstressed, and things should work out just fine." "When do we see you next?" the Invisibles asked. "Normally, I would suggest coming back in a month for another ultrasound," the doctor answered, "but you are a rather unique couple as an ultrasound is completely unnecessary. You already have a womb with a view."

MAMMA MIA, ITS BETTER LATTE THAN NEVER

Francis chained her entire dog walking group outside the Starbucks and made her way inside. She loved the dogs in her care, and Starbucks was a trip she made with the dogs to treat them weekly. The staff thought her a little odd for doing so, but her enthusiasm made serving her a treat. "Hello Francis, what is it today?" the barista asked. "Alrighty, let's see…" Francis said as she stared up at the offerings, "The lab will have a grande macchiato, the poodle would like a grande frappuccino, the beagle a short chai tea and the dachshund will have a white chocolate mocha." "Sounds good, Francis – what size for the mocha?" the barista queried. "Oh my, yes," Francis replied, "The wiener takes it tall."

YOUR WORKING CONDITIONS TRULY DO STINK

The bathroom implements breathed a sigh of relief as the last of the humans left for the day. "Ah, I just feel so gross!" the toothbrush cried out. "Give it a rest, toothbrush," the nail clippers yelled, "at least you get washed off. We're stuck with fingernails, toenails, sometimes even toe jam." This prompted a hearty discussion amongst the entire group as to whose working conditions were the worst. The hairbrush complained about having to be strained through greasy hair. The razor chipped in that being dragged across a face and gagging on shaving cream was no picnic. The loofah whined about being covered in soap and dead skin every day. Everyone had an opinion, and the discussion began getting quite heated, until a small voice could be heard, from the corner of the countertop, saying, "I've got you all beat." Every implement looked to the corner and almost immediately took pity on the deodorant stick, whimpering and shivering to itself. The deodorant collected itself and spoke again, "I've got you all beat, I tell you. I get shoved under their arms and lose a little bit of myself there every day." "Oh man," the emery board said comfortingly, "that really is the pits."

HAUNTED BY A TV,
A BLANKET AND A BOWL OF FROOT LOOPS

Darryl turned up the volume and tore down the street in his classic Mustang. He loved his music almost as much as his car, and he intended for everybody to know it. So up and down the neighborhood, he rolled, blaring his music at ear-shattering decibels. It wasn't conventional music he played. The neighbors might even be forgiving if it was AC/DC, or Rush, or Aerosmith, but it was always an MP3 collection of ghosts singing songs, their eerie voices sending chills down spines. Sure it was the weekend, but he didn't care. Pleasing folks wasn't in his wheelhouse. Rocking out was. And he was rocking out to his Saturday moaning car tunes.

THIS TOPIC IS A LITTLE SKETCHY

Marty looked into the boardroom and sighed. There in the corner, as she had been for the last two months, was the corporate sketch artist. Marty recalled how she had was hired to sketch the events of all meetings by the CEO. Her pictures, along with minutes of the meetings, were supposed to "bring a broader scope of corporate understanding," whatever that meant. But the drawings always made Marty look a little goofy and aloof, and it irritated him to no end. So he grasped his coffee tighter, walked into the room, and sat down in his seat. "Glad you're here, Marty," the CEO said, "we were just discussing our corporate objectives for the next fiscal quarter." "Listen, sir," Marty replied, "I would like to participate, but I do not want to be included in the sketch." "What are you saying, Marty?" the CEO queried. "If I'm going to be part of the sketch, I will not be part of the discussion," Marty countered, "I refuse to be drawn into this conversation."

KEEP IT QUEEN, BOYS

Manuel watched the interview with great interest. The Boss, Bruce Springsteen, was being interviewed live on television, and it was utterly fascinating. There was no stone unturned, no story was off-limits – the interviewer brought the hard questions, and Bruce simply answered in the casual, working man style that endeared him to millions of fans. At one point, he was asked who his biggest fan was. Bruce chuckled to himself and answered, "Well, there's this guy named Juan from Santa Monica who writes me almost every day, has pictures of me all over his room... I'd have to say it's him." Manuel paused the live feed and laughed. Here in Santa Monica, he could think of no bigger fan of Bruce Springsteen than his roommate, Juan Carlos. "Hey, Juan!" Manuel shouted out, "Come here! Bruce Springsteen made a shout out to you on TV!" Juan raced down the stairs, so Manuel rewound the interview a few minutes and replayed the interview answer. "Dang man, it's not me," Juan sighed. "What do you mean, it's not you?" Manuel queried, "You have Bruce Springsteen all over your room, you have Springsteen bedsheets, why you even named your dog Bruce. How is it not you?" "It's not me," Juan answered, "Sure, I'm a huge fan, but I've never actually written him. I'd be too scared that I'd offend him or somethin'. He's probably talking about Juan Gomez, down the street." Manuel took this information in and pondered – Juan Gomez was indeed another big Springsteen fan, enjoyed writing, and likely was the subject. Manuel finally had to concede that another Juan writes the Boss.

"TOTO? TOTO? GET OUT OF THAT AISLE!"

There was still much to do, but the store was getting in shape for the grand opening the next day. It had been Emily's dream to run her own Dollar Store, and finally, it was coming true. She leased the storefront a few weeks back, and since then had been painting, setting up shelving, and making her store a bright, easy to navigate, value shopping mecca for what she was hoping would be a multitude of customers. This was the last task, unpacking all of the store merchandise and deciding where it should go. She had just finished laying out a large selection of collector bowls that proudly honored Queen Elizabeth II's 64 years as monarch to the British Empire when her assistant came by with a large assortment of products. "Where shall I put these?" the assistant queried. Emily replied, "You can put some wares over in aisle 2. You can put some wares on the pegboard at the back of the store, and," she continued as she pointed to the large shelf above her, "you can put some here. Some wares over the reign bowls."

THIS PUN HAS BEEN LED ASTRAY

Visibly rushed, Elsa ran to the elevator and pressed 7. For the third time this week, she was running late for work. Although outside of her control, the boss was starting to get annoyed. She was working out in her head what she had to do for the morning when the elevator suddenly stopped. "What's going on?" she wondered. An elevator stoppage was the absolute last thing Elsa needed today. "Hello, is anyone in here?" a voice crackled through the speaker. "Yes, yes. I'm in here," Elsa replied, "Only me." "Great. Okay, listen," the voice spoke, "you are stuck on the sixth floor. I can get the door open from here, but I can't get you higher than that." Elsa sighed, "That's okay. I'm on seven, so I'll just take the stairs." "Oh, did you not get the memo?" the voice questioned, "the stairs between six and seven are actually under repair this week." Elsa flopped down to the floor, exasperated. How was she going to get to work? "I do have a workaround for you, Miss," the voice offered, "We have asked Rapunzel to come in and work on seven just in case things like this occur." "Great, okay great – sounds good," Elsa got up and answered, "where do I go?" "When I open the door, head to the northwest corner staircase. Rapunzel's long, golden braid is there, so you can use that to go up to seven." So Elsa did as instructed, and as she traversed her way up the braid, all she could think was that the last thing she expected to do would be climbing the hair way to seven.

PAINT IT, FAX

"Sorry, you STILL haven't received it?" Mick asked. It was getting to the point of extreme aggravation. This would mark the fourth time in the last hour that Mick faxed over the sales information, and it still wasn't going through. He knew the fax machine was working – he had sent others this morning – and the fax machine on their side was working as well. "Hey Angie," Mick called over to his workmate, "can you come over here?" Angie came over to the fax machine as Mick continued, "Do you know what's going on? I'm at a loss. I get confirmation printouts that faxes have been sent, I'm even getting printouts that faxes have not been sent, but it's like the fax machine is simply ignoring this number altogether." "Ah, yes," Angie replied, "look here – it's set so that it will only print jobs with a pass or fail status, but not for jobs it ignores outright, and we can't change that setting." "I see," Mick responded, "so even though I've tried, and I've tried, I can't get no status fax shun."

THIS ONE'S JUST FOR THE HALIBUT

"I SAID FISH!!!" Eunice yelled at Jed, her husband of forty years. "Huh?" Jed replied, "What?" "I SAID WE ARE HAVING FISH!!!" she yelled again. It was getting absolutely exasperating. For the last few years, Jed could hear most voices and noises, but his ability to hear anything to do with fish had been rapidly declining. If Eunice said that they were having peanut butter and jelly sandwiches, Jed would get up right away to eat, but if she said tuna sandwiches, no go. If Eunice said we're barbecuing steak, he'd be right there waiting, but if Eunice said we're having salmon, again nothing. She finally walked over to where Jed was sitting and showed him the fish she was preparing for dinner. "Oh, fish!" Jed excitedly said, "I love fish!" Eunice stood there for a moment and finally said, "Look, Jed. I've been telling you we're having fish for dinner for the last ten minutes. It's time, dear. Go get a herring aid."

STRIPES AND STRIPES FOREVER

Jimmy slowly started to wake up. The last thing he remembered was passing out a few hours back. He looked around – he appeared to be in a hospital room but had no idea how he got there. Jimmy struggled to get up, but for some reason, the left side of his body felt very heavy and awkward to move. As Jimmy looked over, his face contorted in horror – the entire left side of his body had been welded to another person! "Wha?!? HELP!!!" Jimmy screamed. The door to the room opened and in walked a doctor. "Ah, Mr. Jamm, you're awake," the doctor casually said. "What the heck is going on?!?" Jimmy yelled out. "It's part of a new program we're trying out," the doctor said, "the young man welded to you is Robert Banks, an inmate at the correctional facility. The hope is that being welded to an ordinary person, like yourself, will help Mr. Banks here function in society." "So I'm welded to a prisoner?" Jimmy queried, "Why? How? Who authorized this? I am so con fused…"

THE LONELY MOOSEHERD

"Dude, seriously, you need to check this out. It's trippy," Gil motioned to Ned. Ned walked over to where Gil was, right by the moose exhibit at the zoo. "Alright, what's up?" Ned asked. "Okay, look over there," Gil said. Ned looked over to where Gil was pointing. Off in the distance, he could see several hilltops, of varying sizes. "So, you see the hilltops, right?" Gil asked. "Yeah, but big deal. They're hilltops, nothing weird there," Ned replied quizzically. "Okay, keep watching…" Gil said. Suddenly Ned heard behind him the sound of one of the moose in the exhibit retching and vomiting. Not something one wants to hear, Ned thought, so he returned his gaze to the hilltops. What he noticed was truly, using Gil's word, trippy. It seemed that as the moose made noises, the hilltops would appear to be straight across horizontally, all one size. "Whoa…" Ned gasped, "That's crazy. The hills are aligned with the sound of moose sick."

WE'LL NEED TO MAKE A GROCERY LISZT

It was a fascinating concept – an entire mall thematically designed around music and musicians. There was a store where one could buy sheet music, another for tuba repairs, a recording studio, a piano shop… if it had to do with music, it was available at this mall. So whenever someone would wander into town and ask if I knew where they could pick up a saxophone, I pointed them towards the Chopin center.

DON'T CRY OVER SPILLED BLUE OYSTERS

"I'm sorry, could you repeat that?" "Yes, sir – the hospital has made a horrible mistake." Dan could hardly understand what he was hearing from the hospital administrator, even after asking for it to be repeated. His wife Ellen was inconsolable, laying in the bed she had been in for nearly fourteen hours giving birth to their first child. Still trying to grasp the situation, Dan stuttered, "So what you're telling us is that you have no idea which baby is ours? That there was a mix-up?" The administrator gulped and replied, "Yes, that's correct. We brought your child into the post-natal care unit, but somehow your child and others had their identification tags misplaced, and now we don't know which child is yours. Our efforts so far to figure it out – DNA testing, blood work, etcetera – have also proven ineffective." Dan sighed, anger raging inside and asked, "So where do we go from here?"

"Well," the administrator said, "We do have one idea if you two are open to it. We have narrowed down your child to be one of two. I can bring them both in, and you can simply select which one you want." Dan looked towards Ellen, and after Ellen gave a confirming nod, he said, "Fine. We'll do that then." The administrator walked out of the room and shortly after returned, holding two babies in his arms. One was happy and content, while the other was wailing and sobbing uncontrollably. "Alright, folks, take your pick," he said. They talked it over and said, "We'll take the quiet, content baby." As the administrator handed the child over, he asked, "Out of curiosity, what made you choose this young man?" "Simple," Dan answered, "I was always taught by my mother that if I ever had to choose between raising a child that was content and one that was crying to choose the content child. Whatever you do, she told me, don't rear the weeper."

ANNIE DREAM WILL DO

Bill yelled upstairs at the top of his lungs, "Christopher, you need to come down here right this minute!" A muffled cry hollered back, "NO!" Bill was exasperated. All he wanted to do was to have a simple chat with his boy. He wasn't in trouble, his grades were good – Bill simply wanted to catch up and see how Chris was doing these days. He rarely spoke, most often grunted replies, so it was difficult to know if he was doing well or not. "I don't know what to do," Bill confessed to Liz, his wife, "He simply won't come down here." "You worry too much," Liz replied, "he will come down in his time. In fact, I know that he has to come down before tonight as he needs a loan to catch a movie with his girlfriend." Bill thought for a moment and said, "So what you're telling me is…" Liz finished off his sentence, "That's right. The son will come out to borrow."

BY JIMINY, COMRADE!

Elena looked out from her hotel room in St. Petersburg and sighed. It was now her fourth day in Russia, and still, her dreams remained just that – dreams. There were so many things she dreamed of – getting married, becoming an astronaut, finishing her novel – but she was no closer to seeing those dreams fulfilled. She stepped away from the window, laid down in her bed, and recounted the words the life consultant told her, making sure she hadn't been missing a step. The words were pretty straight forward though – go to Russia, find the gravesite of a member of the former Russian monarchy, lay down and convulse wildly. She sighed again and made a decision. "Okay, I'll give it one more day," Elena confessed to herself, "I'll try again tomorrow, but if it still doesn't work, I'm going home, with the understanding that maybe dreams don't come true when you twitch upon a czar."

MY LAMA OF MANY COLORS

"You're free to go, Rex," the sheriff said as he held the prison door open. Rex was puzzled – he was a career criminal. There was never a time in his life he was not running from, or jailed by, the law. He was barely even a model prisoner, having instigated numerous riots over the years. Yet here it was – freedom. "Sheriff, I gotta know – why?" Rex asked as he gathered his possessions. "Well, son," the sheriff replied as he held out a little yellow card, "this yellow card came to us from a monastery in Tibet." Rex took the card and looked it over. Although somewhat faded, he could clearly see the words "Get Out Of Jail Free" printed in gold, with his name written underneath. "From what we can gather," the sheriff continued, "it comes straight from the Dalai Lama himself. It's a Dalai Pardon.

I'M RUBBER, YOU'RE... RUBBER TOO?

"Okay, Gail, I'm just going to take these bandages off now," the cosmetic surgeon said calmly. The surgery itself was fairly routine, a means of removing face wrinkles cosmetically, but the recovery took a little longer than anticipated. As the bandages were removed from over her eyes, she slowly opened them ever so slightly, the lights in the room being much brighter than she had remembered. Finally, the bandages were all taken off, and the surgeon held a mirror up for her. "Oh, doctor, you did a marvelous job!" Gail exclaimed joyously, "I look fantastic!" As she gazed upon herself, she noticed that in the room behind her the Michelin Man was also having bandages removed. She put the mirror down and asked, "Isn't that the Michelin Man? I haven't seen him in ages! He looks great!" "Yes, it is," the surgeon replied, "He comes in from time to time to have his rubber skin replaced. He's been retired."

GELATUNE

The conductor was clearly getting frustrated. This was supposed to be a celebration, the 25th anniversary of the city's Philharmonic Orchestra, but due to a fire, they were unable to use their usual recital hall. It meant, then, that an alternative venue would have to be used, but the organizers were having a terrible time tracking one down. Finally, the conductor was waved over by Jane, one of the organizers. "Sir," she started politely, "I have a venue here that is not only available but will seat as many, if not more, attendees than even the recital hall does." "What then is the issue?" he replied tersely, "Book it!" "The problem, sir," Jane replied as she collected herself, "is that there is only a small area to put the orchestra. There is absolutely no way that the full orchestra will fit, let alone have room to play. We'd likely have to remove the strings section altogether." "Bah!" the conductor guffed, "Nonsense. Book it. They will all fit." "But... but..." Jane stammered until the conductor said reassuringly, "listen, young lady. I appreciate your concern, but when I tell you we will fit, we will fit. It doesn't ever seem to matter how large or small the orchestra area is – there's just always room for cello."

SHINY HAPPY PEOPLE

Billy sighed. It was crazy – somehow, a desktop lamp had attached itself to his back, and despite his best efforts, he was unable to remove it. It had to be removed surgically. He sighed again - hospitals made him nervous at the best of times, and now here he was, being prepped for a surgery to remove something he most certainly hadn't expected. His last thought before he went under was a hope that it would prove to be successful. When he awoke, he immediately recognized that the lamp had been taken off. Billy was ecstatic and could barely contain his joy when the doctor came into the recovery room. "Ah, I see you're awake!" the doctor said, "as you can tell, the surgery was a complete success. The lamp is gone. I trust you are happy with the results?" Billy replied excitedly, "Happy? So very, very happy! De-lighted!"

THAT CERTAINLY PUTS A DENTAL IN THINGS

The mood was festive, as you'd expect at Christmas in King Arthur's kingdom of Camelot. Joyful carols rang in the air. Mistletoe adorned every doorway. Every tree was awash in color. The horses wore reindeer antlers in a playful homage to Santa's flying fleet. Leading the festivities were King Arthur himself, along with his Knights of the Round Table. Arthur strode through the village, tossing toys to all of the young ones. Sir Galahad had a cart full of large turkeys, one for each household to have their Yuletide dinner. Merlin ran around conjuring fireworks out of thin air, amazing one and all. Sir Lancelot, being much more practical, would go out of the village and bring dental hygiene products out to the shepherds surrounding the castle. To show their appreciation of this kindness, the shepherds would gather together, hold their hygienic gifts, and parade aloft under Sir Lancelot's room window while calling out their thanks in large, bold voices. While many of these Christmas traditions have been lost over time, we do know that the shepherds did benefit from Lancelot's kindness and did parade by his window, as recounted in the Christmas classic "While Shepherds Walk Their Floss By Knight."

TIKI BELLS

"It's snowing! It's snowing!" Leilani cried, and it was true – despite living in Hawaii, there really was snow drifting down on Christmas Day, covering the beaches and palm trees with a powdery white sheen. From the window, Leilani could see the scores of tourists kicking at the snow and shaking their heads in disbelief, but she didn't care. It was a miracle, and she felt it was just for her. As she threw on her jacket, she ran to her father and asked if she could take Biggles, their Appaloosa horse, out in the snowfall. He laughed as he gave her permission, and she ran out the door. As he looked out at his impulsive daughter, he noticed she had placed both a lasso and a garland of flowers on the saddle before mounting Biggles. He opened the window and asked her what she was doing. "Well, dad," she replied, "the books I've read about winter talk about dashing through the snow on one-horse, rope, and lei."

OH BOY, GEORGE

Jeff looked at his English paper in disbelief. He had never received anything less than a B+ in class, but there it was, his first D-. Shaking, he tiptoed up to his teacher and asked her, "pardon Ms. Smith, but I have to know – what on earth did I do wrong on this paper to deserve such a low mark?" Ms. Smith sighed and took the paper from his hands. She opened it up and began to explain, "well, Jeff, the paper itself was quite good, but there is a complete absence of punctuation marks." "But there ARE punctuation marks, see?" he exclaimed as he pointed to the paper. Ms. Smith took another look, and sure enough, the punctuation marks were there clear as day. "Hmmm," she pondered, "Jeff, this may sound like an odd question, but were you listening to Culture Club when you wrote this?" Jeff thought a moment and replied, "yah, they were on the radio at the time." "I owe you an apology, Jeff," Ms. Smith confessed, "sometimes when a Culture Club song is playing at the same time one writes a paper, the punctuation disappears off and on. You are the victim of a comma chameleon."

DON'T BE BLUE, LAGOON

The advertising executives sat in the boardroom, gazing attentively at the product before them. It was innovative – a small device that attached to the shoe, keeping small streams of water away from the wearer. There was an opportunity to be had – people afraid of water streams, people unwilling to get their shoes wet, wicked witches – the possibilities were endless. All they had to do was come up with an advertising campaign. "How about a catchy slogan, like "getting wet, no need to fret..." Jim started, but he was abruptly cut off by his boss, George. "No, no – I think we need a celebrity to endorse this," George said, "but who? Any ideas? Who could we get to endorse these Brook Shields?"

TAY TAY IS A-OKAY

Bill was frantic. The gala ball was that evening, he had a beautiful young lady to go with, but his favorite dress shirt had somehow been ripped in various locations. It wasn't that Bill couldn't buy a new one, but this shirt was unique. So he raced to the mall, and that's where he saw it – a clothing repair shop that promised repairs completed within five minutes. He entered the Tailors Swift store and asked the owner if his shirt could be repaired. The owner took the shirt in her hands, looked it over, and sadly shook her head no. "Is there anything you can do?" Bill begged. "I'm sorry, sir," she replied, "but this? This is never, ever, ever getting back together." Heartbroken, Bill just stood there, his destroyed shirt in hand. The owner waited a time before asking, "My apologies, but there is something I just have to ask you before you leave. Your singing voice – it's on the higher end, correct?" Bill paused, looked at her with his puzzled face, and said, "why yes, oddly enough it is. How did you know?" The owner replied, "Thought so. I knew you were treble when you walked in."

THIS SHHH JUST GOT REAL

"Watch it!" the colonel cried out, "they could be anywhere here." The war had lasted years. Just when their forces seemed to be in a position to win, the enemy would roll out a new threat that had to be overcome. Their latest weapon was particularly heinous – you couldn't see them as they were buried. You couldn't hear them because they were silent. They were imported from France… And the colonel and his team were walking through an acre of them. They trod carefully, fearful that any step could be their last. Suddenly, private George screamed out as a white-faced character leaped out from the ground, put an imaginary box around him, and killed him before retreating. "Dammit," the colonel grimaced, "I really hate going through these mime fields."

MY NAME'S CLIFF - DROP OVER SOMETIME

It was nearing Christmas, and every child, it seemed, wanted the same thing from Santa. It was a wildly addictive toy and increased interest in geology a thousandfold. Simplistic in its design, all you had to do was to take a picture of a deep ravine or valley, and the toy would create a replica on a smaller scale, in 3D. Because of its popularity, parents were lined up for blocks to buy their children a Gorge Cloney.

ALOE, I LOVE YOU WON'T YOU TELL ME YOUR NAME

Sam was sitting in the bar in Honolulu, Hawaii, enjoying a drink in the island paradise when he spotted a fellow sitting just down from him, head down, and sighing deeply. Not wanting anyone to feel so badly in such a beautiful location, Sam walked over and tapped on the man's shoulder. "Are you okay?" Sam asked. "Not really," the man replied, "I'm having just the worst time." Sam pressed deeper, wanting to know what possibly could be contributing to this man's grief. "The name's Adam," the man said, "and I am a professional comedian for plants. Plants that laugh tend to grow better, and that is my gift. But I am having the worst time with my latest audience, a group of tropical perennial aloe vera plants." "Well, that's certainly an interesting vocation," Sam replied, "but what is the issue with these plants?" "They simply will not laugh at any of my jokes," Adam said, "What I wouldn't give for an aloe ha."

HONG KONG FUEY

The martial arts showcase amazed all of those in attendance. The graceful movements, the powerful chops, the strong kicks, the shattered cinder blocks all presented in a demonstration of the many disciplines. Each one had its unique flair, yet something in it was troubling for Henry. He fully appreciated the art but couldn't shake the feeling that he had seen the whole presentation before. Every chop, every kick, was one that he was positive he had already experienced. "Maybe it's nothing," he thought to himself, "perhaps it's just a feeling of deja fu."

I FIND THE WHOLE THING VERY AMUSEUMING

Scott was livid. He invested a lot of time and money to make the ball caps, each one covered in a print of paintings from the greatest artists of all time. There was a Mona Lisa hat, a Sistine Chapel hat, The Persistence of Memory hat, and so on. He had reasonably priced them, but the government insisted that an additional tax be levied on every item, with no reason that Scott could tell other than to make money. As a result, the cost ended up being significantly higher, damaging his sales. He felt that he had no choice but to hire a lawyer and stand up against the revenue department. He simply had to prevent an art hat tax.

I STILL HAVEN'T FOUND... OH WAIT, THERE IT IS

The weather was simply awful. It had been hailing for hours and didn't appear it was going to let up any time soon. Vehicles and roofing were getting absolutely beat on, forcing people to stay indoors. This proved to be exceptionally troublesome for Arnie Ginn, tour manager for U2. He had gone ahead from their last tour stop to check out preparations, only to find himself stuck inside the hotel. Not wanting the lads to board the tour bus and get caught, he sent them a text advising them to stay put for now. It read, "Trappy hails, U2, until we meet. A.Ginn"

STONE COLD CRAZY

The change in Bob had been a long time coming. Dr. Pepper first met Bob at his psychiatric clinic, back when Bob was in his mid-teens. Bob had been brought in by his mum, who was deeply troubled by the fact that he believed he was a mountain. It was an odd case, sure, but the good doctor was sure that he could help Bob overcome this strange belief. So they began talking, and gradually Dr. Pepper was able to work Bob into believing he was slightly smaller rock formations each time – from mountain to rocky hills, from rocky hills to massive stones, and so on. Now, Bob believed that he was a large rock but was on the cusp of going smaller still. "So what do you say, Bob?" the doctor asked, "do you think maybe we can agree that you are a slightly smaller rock?" Bob panicked momentarily, regained his composure and replied, "I don't think I can today, it scares me. But I do think by tomorrow I'll be a little boulder."

WALK THIS WAY. NO, WAIT. THIS WAY. DEFINITELY THIS WAY.

"HELLO CALGARY!!" Steven Tyler yelled out to the multitude of adoring Aerosmith fans. Yet the concert was significantly different from what the crowd had anticipated. Sure, there was merchandise available in the foyer and the unmistakable odor of mary jane wafting through the building, but on stage, there was only a laptop and a microphone. No Tyler, no Joe Perry, no Brad Whitford – no one from Aerosmith was even in the building. They were, in fact, still in their hotel room, streaming to the venue via Skype. "Sorry we can't be there with you live," Steven continued, "but as we tried to leave this hotel room – this awesome, amazing hotel room – we began crying uncontrollably at the thought of leaving this place, and simply couldn't do it." A hush fell over the crowd as they tried to understand what their rock idol was saying. He continued, "We just love this hotel room so very, very much. Whenever we think we can leave it, we just break down, overcome with suite emotion."

TEEPEE, OR NOT TEEPEE – THAT IS THE QUESTION, LADDY

The video will, containing the last wishes of the recently deceased billionaire Cassius de Posited, had just begun playing. In the room sat Cassius' lawyer and his two children, the only two heirs to his vast fortune. "If you are watching this," Cassius said, "then I have indeed shuffled off this mortal coil and gone to join the choir invisible. I am not pining for the fjords. I am bereft of life." There was a slight pause as he chuckled at his Monty Python reference, and then he continued. "So to my two heirs, I leave all my fortune, to be split between the two of you. You will, however, have to find it. You know I have never trusted banks, and I would never have all of my holdings in a single location." The heirs looked at one another quizzically, then turned their attention back to the screen. "Half has been buried in a vault, located in the depths of a Scottish lake. The other half I entrusted to a First Nations tribe in Alberta, Canada. And there you have it," Cassius stated, "my billions have been kept under loch and Cree."

ONLY FOOLS RUSSIAN

If nothing else, the study group was undoubtedly unique. Composed entirely of chartered accountants from the USSR, they would read pages and pages of historical prophecies that spoke of nothing happening. "The world will not end in 2000." "A mouse named Mickey will not inherit the last five percent of the earth." And so on. One day young Petr, a junior accountant, addressed the group. "Just wondering," he asked, "why don't we ever read about things that will happen? Or even Russian fiction?" The leader of the group stood up and replied, "Petr, while I appreciate your thoughts, I have to be honest. We are all chartered accountants here, and as such, we are only interested in nyet prophets."

OUR LIDS ARE SEALED

The pot luck was in full swing. It was an exclusive event where only 80s bands had been invited. Duran Duran brought meatballs. ZZ Top brought cupcakes. The Thompson Twins brought two appetizers. Culture Club brought fried chicken. Many groups were present, and with that, there was a large variety of pot luck items to choose from. However, despite the excellent turnout, there was a short supply of vegetables. "What'll we do?" the waiting staff asked the organizer, "there are so few veggies on the table." "It's okay," the organizer said, "look over there. The Go-Go's have just arrived. They got the beets."

IT'LL BE RAINING SPOONER OR LATER

"... and the weather this weekend will be," Frank started. He then took a piece of cutlery and hurled it at the wall and claimed, "Sunny. It'll be sunny. Back to you, George." Amazed, the cameraman zoomed in on the wall, where there was a customized poster. The poster was composed of multiple squares, and in those squares were weather descriptions and temperatures. There was a square called "rain," one called "light flurries," one called "59 degrees Fahrenheit" and one called "-4 Celsius", among many others. And where the cutlery landed was in a square called, sure enough, "sunny." When the news broadcast ended, the cameraman approached Frank. He asked, "excuse me, Frank, but I'm fascinated by the weather predictions you make, simply by throwing cutlery at that wall. What's even more interesting is that your accuracy is almost spot-on day after day. How do you do it?" Frank smiled and said, "I come from a long line of people who can tell what the weather is going to be by throwing cutlery at a wall. My great-grandfather could do it. My grandfather could do it. My father can do it, and now I, too, am a weather fork caster."

I'LL HAVE AN EXTRA LARGE DUBLIN DUBLIN

It was the most massive breakout in Irish history. Hundreds of inmates had escaped the prison, a specially designed prison meant to house criminals with severe skin diseases. The warden stood with the chief of police. Both were looking at the empty cells of prison and shaking their heads in disbelief. "I simply don't know how they got out," the warder sighed. The police captain added, "worse yet, we have been utterly unable to find out where they all went." Suddenly Constable O'Malley rushed in to address the two. "Lads," he gasped, "we found them! All of them!" "That's great!" the chief smiled, "but how?" "A wee bit of luck, I'd say," the constable blurted out, "there was a rainbow in the sky, so we followed it to the end, and sure enough, that's where all the leper cons were."

YOU GET A VENTI... YOU GET A VENTI... EVERYONE GETS A VENTI!

Herb walked into his neighborhood Starbucks, as he was wont to do most mornings. Today, however, something was amiss. Everyone inside was covering their ears, looking around for... something. That's when Herb heard it. It started quietly – a gentle knocking sound – but slowly got louder and louder. Just when he himself started covering his ears, the noise stopped. "Weird," he thought as he approached the counter. He was about to order when the knocking sound started again. He asked the cashier, "what the heck is going on?" The cashier, loudly speaking to go over the din, said, "We don't know. It started when we started offering the official Oprah Winfrey saltwater-fish infused chai tea bags." "Ah, don't you see," Herb replied once the sound let down again, "clearly it's Oprah tuna tea knocking."

HUBBA BUBBA TRUBBA

There certainly weren't a lot of groceries. Amy only needed a few things to tide her over to payday – some milk, bread, and a box of cookies, a well-earned gift to herself. So it seemed incredibly odd that the young man bagging the groceries would be having so much trouble. Yet there he was – every time he put something in the bag, his bubble gum would fall out of his mouth. He'd get the gum and put it back in, but still hadn't packed the bag. This cycle continued for a few minutes, and finally, Amy got the attention of the supervisor to see what was going on. As the supervisor came over, she saw what the young man was doing, became very cross, and blurted, "Dammit, Jim – I've told you once, I've told you a million times. Baggers can't be chewers."

YOU DON'T HAVE TO BE CRAZY TO WORK HERE, BUT IT HELPS

Being as close to the sanitarium as it was, St. James' cathedral had to take many precautions to ensure that worship services went as smoothly as possible. It wasn't that the patients at the facility weren't welcome. On the contrary, they had a whole section in the sanctuary where they could participate in the service as they were able. The issue was more with the overall safety of the parishioners. Numerous times the patients would sneak by and sit with the "normals," and this would result in some minor problems, like muttering during the sermon or singing "Sweet Home Alabama," regardless of the hymn that was playing, all the way up to fisticuffs and stolen offerings. To make worship safe and welcoming for everyone, a young lady, Belle, was hired to stand at the back of the church. It was her job to determine who came from the sanitarium and who were general parishioners. To alert ushers about who was to go to each side, it was her responsibility to ring the chimes when a "normal" person arrived, and to simply nod if a patient came in. When asked to describe her job, she answered, "well, I'm ringing in the sane, just ringing in the sane."

I WISH I COULD GOBI THERE

"If you please, sir, follow me," the large Arabian man gestured. Glen got off the motorcycle and walked towards the man who was opening the gate to what appeared to be a large, empty pen. The tour was a bucket list item for sure. Glen had long wanted to take a guided tour across the Sahara desert. Finally, he hopped on a plane and made his way to this dry, arid town on the outskirts of the desert. He was told that the Arabian man, Ahmad, was the best guide around. Ahmad, thrilled with the opportunity to show off the beauty of the desert, grasped Glen on the shoulder and said, "sir – please, feel free to take your choice of animal." Glen peered around, but could not see a single creature – no donkeys, no camels, not even a giant lizard. Thinking Ahmad completely daft, he gently responded, "um… Ahmad, there is nothing here." Ahmad was taken aback. He took a step forward, looked in the pen, and sure enough, he could see nothing. After a moment, a broad smile crept across Ahmad's face, which transformed into loud, boisterous laughing. "My friend, my friend," he chuckled as he turned back towards Glen, "I am so sorry. Here, look." Ahmad walked forward a few paces, reached down, grabbed <u>something</u>, and flipped that something over to the right. And sitting right there, where Ahmad had initially reached, was a large camel. "My apologies again, Mr. Glen," Ahmad said, "I forgot that they were wearing their camel flage."

CANUCK, CANUCK - WHO'S THERE?

Leif was getting angrier and angrier. No matter how hard he pushed, the door simply would not open. "Ja, this is frustrating," Leif exclaimed, "I canst understand why it won't open." Finally, with one last angry shove, he screamed and walked away from it, shaking his head in disbelief. "Well, we needst to get through, ja," Sven spoke, "let me take a lookst." So Sven walked over to the door and began looking it over. He looked at the hinges. He peered over the door handle, he rubbed his hands over the door jamb, carefully inspecting each thing on and around the door to no avail. Finally, he noticed in the very top right corner, a small engraving that read "Made In Canada." "Ja, I've got it!!" Sven joyfully exclaimed. "Whatst is it, Sven?" Leif asked. "Well, the door was made in Canada," Sven replied, "so while it might push open, it's far more likely that it may pull, Leif."

HEY YOU - YES, YOU. SMARTEN UP. STOP BEING COMFORTABLY DUMB

Before Belle arrived at the Beast's castle, the mood was decidedly dour. Each day came with less and less hope that the people within the castle would escape their current fates, remaining changed to household items for the rest of their lives. This knowledge weighed heavily on everyone, and from time to time, emotions would rise, resulting in arguments, shouting, and even fighting. Today was particularly bad – the Beast was sporting a headache, and his anger and pain were palpable, putting everyone on edge. Tiptoeing around so as not to make things worse, Lumiere, the candle, made his way to the kitchen. However, an errant misstep resulted in him bumping into Brutus, the frying pan. Tempers flared, and suddenly the two became engaged in a fist-flying dustup of epic proportions. So much so that the Beast came down from his room. Surveying the situation, the Beast was about to pull the combatants apart when he suddenly just walked away. "Bah, it's not worth the hassle," the Beast thought to himself, "it's a frying pan and just another wick in the brawl."

ONE, TWO FREDDY'S COMING FOR –
OH, HE'S HERE ALREADY. YO FRED, WHASSUP?

It was a bad time for the letter L. Recently, the letter L had been blamed for sorcery and witchcraft in the village. Any words or names containing the letter were forced to drop L in favor of a different letter, perhaps a Q or Z. Things were getting so bad in fact that no one was even using the letter in discussion, merely calling it "the etter that can not be named." Word from the village finally made it's way up to Sir Lancelot, who was recently elected mayor of the region. Realizing just how absurd the whole abuse of a single letter was, he called together the council for a quick meeting. "Gentlemen," the mayor started, "the letter L can't possibly be the cause of such ills in our village. I propose we have a town meeting where I can talk about this." And so the meeting was scheduled for that evening, with posters encouraging the villagers to come and hear the Knight Mayor on L Mistreat.

FOLLOW YOUR NOSE, IT ALWAYS KNOWS. UNLESS IT DOESN'T AND IT'S A SILLY NOSE

"Seriously, it's right there," the duo sighed together as they pointed to an area in the cereal aisle of the local grocery store. "I'm sorry, I just do not see any Froot Loops," the young man replied, "I see Cap'n Crunch, Tony the Tiger on the Frosted Flakes, Snap, Crackle and Pop on the Rice Krispies, but I do not see any Froot Loops boxes, let alone the Froot Loops mascot." The two clerks looked at one another in disbelief. They could see boxes and boxes of Froot Loops right in front of their faces, yet the shopper was adamant he could not. "Well, let me talk to the manager," the taller clerk stated as he began to walk away. As he turned around the corner, though, his partner yelled out, "Holy crap – they've disappeared! The Froot Loops have disappeared!" The clerk ran back, but as he sidled up to his partner, he said, "well, that's weird – now I can see them again." The clerk pondered a while, and then his face lit up. "Got it!" he burst out, "a single person can't see the Froot Loops or its mascot while a duo can. It's so obvious – one can't, but two can."

"AND A COLD FRONT COMING IN FROM THE JEST..."

The movie had finally gone through final rewrites and had begun the process of filming. The plot of the film had four main characters, all circus clowns, and their experiences during a typical day at the circus. However, the four actors were less than impressed with the rewrites as they felt the script now felt one-dimensional and boring. So they approached the director and expressed their concerns. He listened intently and said, "you know, I have to admit you are right. What would you suggest to make the film more interesting?" The four actors huddled together, chatted amongst themselves, and turned back to the director. "Maybe," one said, "it would be more interesting if we were still clowns, but had mood disorders." "I like it," the director applauded, "I think we could do a lot with clowns that went from happy to angry in a split second." "Agreed," another added in, "but if we go down that path, do you think we could bring in some clowns that DO have mood disorders for research?" "I don't see why not," the director replied. He picked up his cell phone, checked his contacts, and called the producer. "Johnny, Johnny," the director began, "I have four cast that are calling for clowny with a chance of furies."

THE FONT-ING OF YOUTH

The rowdy font types piled into the saloon, cursing, shouting, and laughing heartily at the destruction they were causing with the local documents. As they continued pouring in, they became more and more demanding. Arial font demanded whiskey. Calibri Light wanted a sasparilla. Gill Sans Ultra Bold grabbed a bottle of rum from behind the counter and poured it on the floor, bending down to lick it up to the childish delight of Lucida Handwriting. Suddenly, the door swung open, and the whole saloon went quiet. They couldn't quite make out who it was, but heard loud and clear the deep bellow, "I reckon you'd best be on your best behavior or get out of my word processor now." "Who are you?" Albertus Extra Bold asked. "I'm the law around these parts," came the answer, "I'm the new serif in town."

THIS BAKERY HAS BEEN AUTHORIZED

You could smell the delightful aroma of the bakery from blocks away. It had only opened a week ago but was already a popular destination, thanks in large part to its unique spin on baked goods. You see, on everything that they made, an excerpt from a famous author was placed on top. The rye bread had a quote from Shakespeare – "To be or not to be." "It is our choices, Harry, that show what we truly are, far more than our abilities" from Rowling's "Harry Potter and the Chamber of Secrets" could distinctly be read on the gingerbread. From Stephen King's "The Shawshank Redemption" came, "Fear can hold you prisoner. Hope can set you free," as read on the baguettes. Today, though, was especially exciting for the staff as Paul McCartney had come in for the third time that month to pick up some more of his favorite selection, which read atop "When I die, I hope to go to heaven, whatever the hell that is." It was perhaps to be expected, of course, that McCartney would prefer to have Rand on the bun.

DON'T MENTION THE WAR

The phone rang abruptly, prompting Principal Miller to take the call straight away. Expecting to begin with pleasantries, he was taken aback at the venomous onslaught that came from the other end. "What the heck are your social studies teachers teaching our kids?!?" it began. Principal Miller covered the phone, sighed, and returned to the call. "My apologies, sir," he replied, "but I'm not sure what it is that you are referring to. If you can just calmly tell me..." "What do you mean you're not sure?!?" the parent interrupted, "do you have no <<bleep>> concept of what's taught in your classrooms?!?" Dozens of schedules and learning plans raced through his mind as he struggled to understand the source of the parent's anger. He started again. "If I'm not mistaken, the social studies students are currently learning about Germany, more specifically Germany in World War II. Is that what this is about?" A loud sigh was heard, followed by, "yes, that IS what this is about. Why?!? I don't think it should even be a topic of discussion, let alone education!! I'll be damned if my kid learns any more about Adolf Hitler!" Principal Miller collected this information, thought a moment, and said, "so if I understand correctly, you are mad because the students are learning about Hitler?" "Not just mad," the parent replied, "I'm absolutely Fuhrerous."

YOU'RE NOT TO BRIGHT

Josh was a little perplexed. He specifically went to the local Dunkin' Donuts to grab a snack and use the free wi-fi to complete his schoolwork. When he got there, the store inside was brightly lit. Yet as soon as he ordered his Mountain Dew and a honey cruller, the lights diminished to such a degree it was difficult even to find his table. Stumbling to the counter, Josh demanded to speak to the manager. "Look, man," Josh began, "I came here to do some work, but now it's so dark in here I can barely make out the words in my book." The manager apologized and asked what Josh had ordered, so Josh showed him the goods he had just bought. The manager glanced, grimaced slightly, and said, "Again, I am sorry, sir, but you bought a Mountain Dew and a donut." "So?" Josh replied quizzically. "Well," the manager responded, "you're dimmed if you Dew and you're dimmed if you donut."

I MEAN YOU NO H-ARMY

"Mister President," John, the senator from Denver Colorado, began, "there is supposed to be a separation of church and state. So why are we moving forward with this initiative?" The initiative in question was a move by the President to have pictures of Christian temples, ones specifically honoring Jesus Christ, placed on the sleeves of all military uniforms. It was one of many divisive actions of late, but at present, the one with the most negative press. The secretary of state leaped to his microphone, "how dare you, sir," he angrily defended, "how dare you question the President like this!!" Instantly the atmosphere in the room became uncomfortably tense. After a few minutes in silence, the President himself arose to address the room. "Thank you for trying to defend me, mister secretary," he began, "but it is unnecessary. As for your question, senator, it is quite simple and admittedly selfish on my part. Son shrines on my soldiers make me happy."

IT WAS THE WONG THING TO DO

The pile on the front lawn continued to grow every minute. Objects came flying out of the front door, adding to the monstrous mountain of stuff—all different, yet similar in their Asian flavor. There was fine china, Hello Kitty merchandise, jade statues of Buddha, ramen noodles and chopsticks were just a few of the items littering the yard. One neighbor managed to walk through the front door in between the barrage of Asian goods being thrown outside, only to find the owner of the home, Bill, in a frenzied state. He was looking everywhere for anything that could even remotely be Asian. She called out to Bill, encouraging him to calm down, and when he had, she politely asked, "Bill, I'm not sure what's going on here, but are you feeling okay?" Bill settled himself down and replied, "yes, yes, I'm feeling fine. Just a little dis-Oriented."

A RATHER OZ-PICIOUS OCCASION

"It's another one, Sarge," the constable said, "just under the sheet." Sergeant Jones walked over to the crime scene, lifted the sheet, and sure enough, the victim died the same way as dozens of others in the Topeka area. A serial killer was on the loose - that he was sure of, and he had a pattern. Every night there was a full moon the killer struck, leaving behind nothing but rope fibers around the victim's necks. This time was different, though. The killer also left behind a small piece of metal that clearly came from a Toro lawnmower. He pondered over this and called the constable over. "I think I might just have it," the sergeant said, "It sounds crazy, but I think we're dealing with the supernatural here. I've heard of stories but assumed they were a myth, stories about lawnmowers that turn into tangled pieces of murderous rope at the sight of the full moon." The constable took it in, sighed, and replied, "you're right, Sarge, it is crazy but quite honestly the only thing that makes any sort of sense. What should we do?" "I want a full media blitz," Sergeant Jones said authoritatively, "I want the public to be on the lookout, to be safe. I want a warning sent out right away – social media, newspapers, posters, newscasts…" The constable took out his notepad and said, "sure enough – what should it say?" Sergeant Jones thought a moment and said, "Were-Knot in Kansas – Any Mower."

YOU GIVE EXISTENTIANILISM A BAD NAME

Jon Bon Jovi walked up to the stage, grabbed the microphone, and stood silently for a moment. He and his band, Bon Jovi, had played many arenas and stadiums in the past. Today, however, he was on his own, launching a publicity tour for his new philosophy book. The book was a passion project, a collection of his philosophical outlooks on life. "Thank you all for coming," Jon began, "I'm happy to take questions now." The questions were rather simple to start with – when did he come up with the idea for a book, is there a new album coming out, will you sign this for my daughter, why is the book cover red, and so on. Finally, one reporter stepped up to the microphone and asked, "I've read your book, Jon, and it is absolutely fascinating. I do have a question on chapter 14 – you wrote that to know you're alive, that you exist, go to the grocery store. If there are rows of groceries there, you must then exist. Care to clarify?" Jon smiled, clearly impressed at the nature of the question, and replied, "it's easy, man – just remember "Aisle B, therefore you."

COME ON BARBIE, LET'S GO PAWNING

Jenny needed money, and soon. The cost for repairs to her car was significantly higher than expected, so between that and the Christmas presents she still had to buy, she simply didn't have enough to cover it all. So Jenny returned home and looked around. "Maybe there's something here I can pawn," she mumbled to herself as she went through the boxes downstairs, still in need of unpacking from her last move. One box she opened had her vast collection of Barbie dolls. She stared at them – there were a lot of dolls in there, some of which were collector items that could be worth quite a bit. Jenny hated the thought of parting with them, but desperate times called for desperate measures.

She closed the box again and took it to the nearest pawn shop, where she emptied the box and asked the curator what she might get for them. He looked them over and said, "nothing. These are worthless, and we simply do not take Barbie dolls here. You'll have to leave." He threw the dolls back in the box, shoved the box back towards Jenny, and ushered her out the door. Jenny stood outside, in disbelief of what had just happened to her. The more she thought about it, the more upset she became. The tears started slowly, but soon they sprang from her eyes like waterfalls, joined by the sound of uncontrollable sobbing. She went back inside the pawnshop and put the box down on the counter again. In between her howls of weeping, she managed to ask, "won't you please reconsider?" The owner, clearly uncomfortable at this point, replied, "yes, yes, I will - $1000, but please stop!!" Jenny took the money, wiped her tears away, and managed a "thank you" before heading out the door again. She was overjoyed – it was over and above what she needed, and all it took was to hock the dolls with howls of bawling.

DOES ANYBUNNY KNOW WHAT'S GOING ON HERE?

Jim was having a hard time. Here it was, the evening of December 31st, and he had just lost his pet bunny Hoppy. He knew it was crazy to be so saddened by the loss, but Hoppy was special. Hoppy could look at a picture of an ear and identify exactly who or what it belonged. Big ones, long ones, small ones – it didn't matter. Hoppy could identify them all, and now he was gone. As the time clicked ever closer to midnight, Jim stood up, cleared his throat, and addressed the crowd at the party. "Hi, everyone," Jim began, "I know we're having a party here, and I don't want to be a downer, but my bunny Hoppy passed away earlier this week." Jim stopped to wipe away a tear that had started to roll down his cheek and continued, "so tonight I'd ask you to remember Hoppy, and how Hoppy knew ears."

OZ-LA-DI, OZ-LA-DA

Todd carefully lifted the book and blew the dust off. He couldn't believe his luck – in his hands was an original first-draft handwritten copy of L. Frank Baum's "The Wizard of Oz." As he gently thumbed through the pages, he realized that there was a chapter in this draft that wasn't included in the final released version of the book. Titled "Scarecrow's Story" the section went into great detail about the Scarecrow's history. As Todd read through, he learned that the Scarecrow loved beetles, was once named Barry, and how he had deep empathy for a young girl named Ava who had visited Oz years before Dorothy's arrival. It was the last point that Todd found fascinating. He had never known that Straw Barry feels for Ava.

QUIT MAKING ALL THAT RACKET, SHEEP

Jimmy Kimmel laughed in disbelief. Here was Bruce Springsteen, one of the most excellent musicians of all time, and he had just told a story that was too insane to believe. "So, Bruce, let me get this straight," Jimmy started as he collected himself, "you say you have a pet sheep that is so smart it writes columns for newspapers and magazines. You'll forgive me if I'm a little skeptical." "It's alright, Jimmy, it's alright," Bruce replied, "I know it sounds crazy, but I swear it's true. She just finished a piece for the ESPN website on great tennis players. I didn't have a chance to look at it before she sent it in, though – I know she was torn about who to write about. It was between Bjorn Borg and John McEnroe." "Let's look then," Jimmy exclaimed as he turned his laptop on and went to the ESPN site, "riiiight... here. Holy crap, it's true! And it looks like it's Bjorn in the ewe's essay."

THAT STRIKES ME AS BEING VERY COD

"I swear to you," Bill implored as he sat down, "the fish was honestly four feet long." Sally shook her head. It wasn't the first time Bill had returned home from a fishing trip and wasn't the first time that he had nothing to show for it but a story about how large the "one that got away" was. "four feet? That's pretty big," Sally slowly replied, "bigger than the three last month and the eight-footer last year." "Right?" Bill quickly stated back, "it's such a shame that they all got away." At that, Bill got up and moved towards the washroom to freshen up. Sally stood in disbelief and knew that she had to find out if it was true or not. She picked up her cell and texted Frank, who was also on the fishing trip. Upon seeing his reply, Sally turned red with rage and stormed towards Bill. "Look at this!!" she yelled, "Frank says not only didn't you catch a fish this weekend, but the largest fish you ever caught was 6 inches long, tops. I think you're a halibutual liar!"

MAY THE FORCE BE WITH YOU, AND DON'T PAY TIL 2025

Herb looked at the price tag and couldn't believe his luck. The furniture store had an official Star Wars couch, peppered with images from all of the films and lightsabre holders, and it was marked at $12.99. Herb called the sales representative over and said, "I'll take this!" The rep picked up the price tag and shook his head. "Good grief," he muttered, "of all the…" "Is something wrong?" Herb asked, knowing full well it was marked well below cost. "Yes," the rep sighed, "the new warehouse guy put the wrong price tag on this. But that's what you see, and that's what we'll sell it to you for. We'll chalk this up to a Wookie mistake." Herb was thrilled, but these days it was hard for him to scratch up $12.99, so he asked, "can I pay some now and the rest later?" The sales rep said, "yep. We can put it on Leia-way for you."

THE GOOD OLD HAUNTY GAME IS THE BEST GAME YOU CAN NAME

Bobby sat fearfully in the penalty box. Ever since his trade to the Blackhawks, Bobby had been followed around by a ghost during each hockey game. It was, by most accounts, not malevolent but still unnerving. Bobby got so worked up over this that he had started to develop large non-cancerous infections on his rear end, making it difficult even to sit. The coach looked over at Bobby from the bench and turned to his assistant. "Poor Bobby. What do you think we should do?" Coach asked. "I don't know – maybe pull him from the rest of the game?" the assistant replied. The coach shook his head and said, "We probably should, but he already has a ghoul and an ass cyst."

THE RAIN IN SPAIN FALLS PLAINLY ON THE MAINE

"Hm – I don't see what I want on this menu," Eldon stated as he looked the menu over, "I'm hankering for some sandpaper." "That's a very odd request," the server replied, "but it just so happens that the chef ordered some sandpaper in, and it's one of the specials tonight." Eldon was elated. "Wonderful!" he exclaimed, "but may I ask where it's from?" "Just a moment, sir, and I'll find out for you," she said as she walked towards the kitchen area. Patiently Eldon waited until the server came back and said, "it's a sandpaper that comes from Portland – very rare, but delicious." With that, Eldon slammed his menu shut and said, "well, that's perfect! So I'll have a glass of water, some calamari for an appetizer, and then the Portland sandpaper as the Maine course."

SIX LETTERS, STARTS WITH A P

The doctor and the nurse looked Ann over up and down, yet still couldn't figure out what was wrong with her. She came to Emergency last night, complaining of feeling like a fifteen across and a twelve down. It was a symptom that the staff on the late-night shift had never heard before. Although the team looking at her now specialized in difficult diagnoses, they too were at a loss. "How are you feeling this morning?" the doctor asked as the nurse took down her vitals. "A little better – more like a nine across and a four down," she replied. "I have to be honest with you, Ann," the doctor said defeatedly, "in all my years I have never come across symptoms like yours. I just do not know what it could be." Ann shrugged and said, "I get it – I've tried looking it up on the internet myself and have found nothing. I'm puzzled."

ELTON JOHNNY B. GOODE

"C'mon, try it!" Marilyn encouraged her friend Diana, "honestly, it's sooooo good!" Diana was skeptical, of course – the only pickles she had only ever tried were from a jar, and she had to admit that she didn't even really like them. Yet here was Marilyn, standing in the field with her hair billowing in the breeze, holding an open tin of pickles and thoroughly enjoying every one. With a sigh of defeat, Diana walked over to Marilyn. She knew Marilyn was relentless, and if she didn't try them now she would never hear the end of it. Marilyn was thrilled that Diana had come over, and said to her, "okay, now just stand on this rock so you can feel the breeze. When you're ready, take a pickle from the tin and eat it." So Diana stood there a moment, took a pickle and ate it. Sure enough, it was the most amazing thing she had ever eaten, and as she reached for more she happily shouted, "you were right, Marilyn – I love canned dill in the wind."

AMNESIA? NO, YOU'RE THE NESIA

Phil was terribly afraid as he walked into the doctor's office. The affliction had started just over a week ago but had already exacted a toll on his fragile psyche. As his name was called, he got up, walked toward the examination room, and waited patiently. The doctor came into the room within minutes, introduced himself, and asked, "So, Phil – what brings you in today?" "Well, doc, it seems that every time I... sorry, just a moment... AHCHOO!!" Phil sneezed loudly. It took him just a moment to collect himself, and then he resumed talking. "Sorry, doc – what were we just talking about?" Phil questioned. "Hm... I asked you what brought you in today to see me," the doctor replied. "I'm so sorry," Phil said apologetically, "it's just that every time I sneeze I seem to be losing memories, losing the things I've learned over the years. I have even had my Mensa membership revoked as my IQ keeps lowering with every episode." The doc wrote all of this down, assessing the situation before him. Finally, he spoke, "let me assure you, Phil, that we can stop and reverse the effects. What you have is Auto Expelled Limbic Regression. Basically, you're blowing your knows."

SIMON (AND GARFUNKEL) SAYS

"And finally, the last stop on our tour," the guide said as she motioned towards the large plaque before her. "What is it?" someone from the back shouted. "Glad you asked," the guide replied, "you can see this elaborate bridge here?" The tour group looked over and agreed that yes, they could see the bridge. The guide continued, "the plaque here tells the story of why this commemorative bridge was built. Way back in 1962, a group of athletes were jogging down this very path, only to arrive at this point. There was no bridge at the time, so they had to try and cross the stream. Unfortunately, at the same time, there was a rock slide roaring down from the mountain here. The joggers were unable to get out of the way and tragically died under piles of rock and debris. The bridge was built in their memory." "Oh," one of the ladies in the group began, "so what you're saying is..." The guide interrupted her and said, "yes – this is a bridge over rubbled trotters."

I NEED TO USE THE WATERLOO

The beach was full of them, seagulls that were singing popular music. They were singing so well in fact that one could easily have thought that someone had their Spotify playlist cranked to 11. The scientific community took note almost immediately, and a group had arrived at the beach to check the birds out. They were able to capture one humanely and brought it into their research van for closer inspection. One of the scientists drew some blood from the musical bird and looked at it under the microscope. After some time, he moved away from the microscope and said, "I think I know how they're able to sing. Take a look at this." After each member of the team had a chance to look at the sample, the scientist began, "you all see it too, right?" They all nodded in agreement, and one piped up, "so obvious – the DNA indicates that these birds come from Sweden. They are ABBAtrosses."

TAKE HIM TO THE BIRD UNIT, STAT

The donation to the animal hospital was very, very generous, and the construction of the gifted hospital wing began almost immediately. It would gather together experts in the field of bird care, welcoming any injured or dying birds from all over the world. It started successfully, with every flying creature from canaries to parrots being brought in for care. As time dragged on, however, the only birds being brought in were penguin-like, injured out at sea. Finally, the hospital staff gathered together to discuss their next options for the area. "We certainly can leave the area open for all birds," the chief administrator began, "but it has become a very auk ward."

HE AIN'T HEAVY. HE'S MY...
HOLY CRAP, HE IS HEAVY

Jared's mom had Jared stand against the wall, took out her pencil, and marked out his height this year. "Just look at that, Jared," his mom said with tears of happy memories streaming down her face, "just look at how you've grown! And now you're the tallest one in the family!" Jared forced a smile, but inside he felt defeated. He had been dreading this day for years, doing whatever it took to try NOT to grow taller, but finally he had eclipsed his older brother Eric's height by a good three inches. It wasn't the fact he was tallest that bothered him, of course, but it was the responsibility of the tallest in the family to pull their father around in his transport cart. Jared loved his dad and would do anything for him, but he saw the aches and pains Eric had over the years due to pulling the wagon and, selfishly, he simply didn't want to have the same. But the day had come. Jared walked over to where his dad was sitting and said, "Hey dad, it looks like I'm your new transport guy." His dad smiled broadly, exclaiming, "that's wonderful! I do appreciate this, you know." "I know, dad," Jared replied, giving in to the rule that the bigger you are, the father you haul.

MAYBE A DINGO ATE YOUR GRAVY

"… and the colors have to be seen to be believed! Deep pinks, purples, vibrant greens…" the presenter continued. Bruce sighed. He had accepted the "Celebrate Australia" dinner invitation happily, but as time went on, he started to regret it more and more. It's not that it wasn't interesting. The first ten minutes of the presentation on the Great Barrier Reef was fascinating. It was the fact that it was now ninety minutes in, and the presenter was still going on about how great the Great Barrier Reef was. Suddenly a thought occurred to him, and he whipped the dinner invite out of his pocket, looked it over, and when he found what he was looking for, he slumped back in his chair. "Darn it," he thought to himself, "I thought for sure it was a typing error, but there it is – "You've are invited to a boast Reef dinner."

IF YOU'RE WONDERING WHO'S MAKING DINNER, IT'S SMEE

Christie was a huge Disney fan, and by all accounts she was also a fantastic cook. She buzzed through Disneyland like a child, looking amazed at all the sights it held for her, laughing hysterically as each ride exploded joy in her heart. Finally, her trip was winding down, and as she had resolved to do upon arriving she hit the stores to buy Disney merch before heading home. Christie picked up the typical souvenirs – mouse ears, plushies, t-shirts – but what she was hoping to find was Disney cookware. She scoured every store until she finally hit one in Fantasyland that did indeed carry cookware. As she looked them over, she marveled at the craftsmanship, with each handle embossed with the Disneyland logo and a headshot of Mickey Mouse. However, she noticed that each piece of cookware was made from a silver-gray tin alloy. It seemed an odd choice, and she was really hoping for stainless steel, but then it occurred to her – this was Fantasyland, so of course they would be pewter pans.

WHAT THE PUCK IS GOING ON HERE?

"It's a disaster, gentlemen," the NHL commissioner began his address to the general managers, "this virus is attacking every one of our hockey players." They all shook their heads, wanting to believe the best, but knowing it was now a worst-case scenario before them. "I'd like to introduce you to Dr. Hipsheck," he continued, "the doctor who has been monitoring the situation. Please, sir, if you would." The doctor walked up to the head of the table and began his explanation. "What we have here is a virus that, for some reason, is only impacting hockey players," Dr. Hipsheck stated as he shuffled his papers, "and it's a virus with bizarre symptoms. Those affected become covered in pimples, in sores. This alone isn't strange, but what is strange is that these sores are filled with drearily commonplace Red Rose orange pekoe tea." "Can it be cured?" the Flames general manager queried. Dr. Hipsheck smiled as he answered, "that's the good thing. These events only last for 10 minutes before going away. Odd, yes, but it's only 10 minutes in the banal tea pox."

WHAT A NOVEL CONCEPT

"I'll be honest, I had expected these would be much more popular," Jim said to his business partner as he pointed to the toys before him. In his defense, the concept was fascinating. It was a line of stuffed toys representing famous books. There was a stuffed "War And Peace," a stuffed "To Kill A Mockingbird," a stuffed "The Hunger Games," and so on. Despite a massive marketing push, the stuffies just never did catch on with the public, forcing toy stores to place them in bargain bins for $1 apiece. "Don't be too hard on yourself," his partner chimed in, "I also thought there would be more love for plushable toy lits."

CANOE REPEAT YOURSELF, PLEASE?

Sarah gently nudged Jim awake. "Jim, Jim, wake up," she said. As he stirred awake, the memory of the ordeal they had just been through flashed through his mind. One minute they were navigating the rapids in their canoe, and the next they were tossed out, forced to swim for their lives to the nearest riverbank. Exhausted, both briefly fell asleep. Sarah had been up for a little while, assessing their situation, and now Jim stood up to join her. "I built a fire," Sarah let him know, "go get warmed up." As Jim gladly stood by the warmth of the fire, he looked around. There was the canoe – a little banged up but otherwise in good condition. A handful of their supplies had been salvaged, including energy bars he had insisted on bringing in the first place. "Well, Sarah, I guess we have no choice – we'll have to go back into the river and paddle back to civilization," he said. Sarah shook her head. "No, Jim," she sadly said, "the canoe is fine, but the paddles are gone. They went flying to the other side of the valley, the one to the right." Jim began to walk over to see what it would take to cross the valley to retrieve the paddles when he noticed that they were not across the valley but instead leaned up behind a tree nearby. "Sarah, they're right here," Jim quizzically said. "I know," Sarah replied sheepishly, "I lied. They were never across the valley. They've been here the whole time." Jim stood in disbelief. "Seriously?" he finally blurted out, "you faked an oar chasm?"

Pun and Grimeish Mint   117

LED (ZEPPELIN) ASTRAY

Robert was becoming more and more frustrated as time went on. He knew the hotel he was staying at was adjoined to the multi-level high-end fashion store and that an entrance to the hotel was somewhere in the store. But despite walking through every level and every department, he could not find it. Finally, he came across an employee of the store. "Pardon me," Robert asked the sales associate, "I can't seem to find the entrance to the hotel. Can I trouble you for directions?" The associate looked at him sympathetically and replied, "I'm so sorry, sir – it is not easy to find." She stopped briefly and pointed behind Robert to the left before continuing. "If you walk that direction, you'll come across our discount area, where we sell name-brand fashions that are no longer in style. Head towards the wall to the left – you'll find the Inn through the out Dior."

NAÏVE, THE NIGHT BEFORE NAIDAY

Ashton stood at the foot of the hospital bed. There lay his good friend Stu. Ashton and Stu had been inseparable from the first day of grade 1, the best of best friends. They joked around with each other all the time. Stu was always pulling practical jokes on Ashton. Ashton, in turn, took full advantage of Stu's gullibility, making him believe in the most skeptical of claims, like the time he convinced Stu that he found a whole herd of unicorns. As time went on, the practical jokes and outlandish stories waned, but the friendship did not, so as soon as he heard that Stu was going to the hospital because he had lost all sense of touch and feeling Ashton was on the first flight he could find home. It helped Ashton immensely to see that Stu was able to get some sleep, at least. He was just about to sit when a nurse came in. "Oh, I'm sorry," the nurse apologized, "I didn't realize Stu had a visitor. Are you family?" Ashton smiled a bit and said, "pretty much – Stu is a numb buddy that I used to snow."

DON'T STOP THEM, I SAY SPACE-TIME CONTINUE-EM

The night had finally arrived – the big fundraising concert to raise money for Michael J. Fox's "Fight Parkinsons" initiative. The orchestra was prepared to play many classical compositions, and invites went out to all of the business chairpersons in the area. However, as time wore on, it became clear that only a handful of the chairpersons invited were coming. The orchestra was downhearted – they had expected a full house, but instead would be playing to one of the smallest crowds they had ever seen. Picking up on their disappointment, both Michael J. Fox and Christopher Lloyd, who was here helping his friend out, walked over and began talking to the musicians. "Look," Michael began, "I know it's not a lot of people, but we can still entertain them. Let's cut the program back a bit and just play some pieces from one composer or so." "Like what?" the burly tuba player bellowed. Christopher chimed in, "well, maybe we could just play Bach to the few chairs."

LOOKS LIKE SOMEBODY HAS A CASE OF THE MOONDAYS

It was bold and more than a little bit dangerous, but that wasn't going to stop Dr. Acula from what would be his most significant scientific feat in the field of genetics. For months he gathered DNA from history's greatest monsters and maniacs - sea monsters, vampires, serial killers, golems, and giant ants, to name a few. In the hope of creating a creature that was not only scary but could potentially be used for military purposes. To date, every combination he tried failed miserably, the YetiBlob being the most recent effort. Today, though, looked promising. He took the DNA from the Invisible Man and combined it with the DNA of a lycanthrope, and so far, testing was positive. All that was left was injecting the sample into his assistant Igor, which he did with skeptical optimism. Suddenly, Igor began growing hair, claws, and sharp teeth before disappearing altogether. "Eureka, I've done it!" the doctor shouted, "I've created the first where-wolf!"

LOOK WHO'S TOLKIEN NOW

"Okay, so now I want Frodo to hit Samwise with the pie!" the director shouted, "aaaaaand... action!" When the actors were done, he shouted, "cut! Excellent – now, Peregrin, hit Meriadoc in the head with that hammer. Aaannnd... action!" Again the actors performed the scene as instructed. Throughout the day, they were directed to do the most outlandish slapstick for the film. There were pies in the face, eye pokes, hits in the head with various objects, for example. Finally, the actor playing Frodo walked up to the director and said, "we've been doing this all day, sir. Haven't you got enough for the film? What exactly is the film even about?" The director paused, looked at his watch, and replied, "oh no, I'm so sorry. I didn't realize how much time had passed. I got quite carried away with these humorous scenes – it's a farce of Hobbit."

MANELY IN FINLAND

Vic was perplexed. It was a long marathon, and it was only after a few hours that the first few runners made it to the end. However, one by one they would go over and slap the lion that was off to the side, angering it before their official time was recorded. When there was a pause in the race, Vic walked over to one of the marathon officials. "Excuse me, may I ask why each runner is slapping that lion?" he inquired. "Ah, yes," she replied, "the lion is Hannu Lienkammen, on loan from the Helsinki zoo. For the race to be completed, each participant has to do what they can to make him angry." The light came on for Vic. "Oh, I see," he stated, "before they post their time, they need to cross the Finnish lion."

A ROLLING STONE GATHERS NO MOSSCOW

Many years had passed since Santa last visited the boys and girls in Russia. It certainly wasn't anything that they had done – heaven knows most of them would have ended up on the nice list – but he so strongly disagreed with communism that he refused even to step foot in the country. In fact, it had been so long that he was reasonably sure that most of the population wouldn't even know who he was. One day his administrative elf rushed into his office. "Santa, Santa!" he exclaimed, "you've gotta see this!!" With that, he dropped his laptop onto Santa's desk and showed Santa the YouTube video that was going viral. Thousands of Russians were gathered together, all holding signs echoing the same sentiment – they wanted communism to end, but most importantly, they wanted Santa to come back. Wiping away a tear Santa let out a hearty Ho Ho Ho before asking the elf where he found it. "Well, Santa, I was just on my break, so was surfing the net," he began, "when I started seeing a lot of feeds about it. I went to YouTube, and sure enough, I saw commies missing Santa Claus."

ENOUGH OF THESE REINDEER WINTER GAMES

Otto was furious. He had been sound asleep when Dolph crawled into his room with a shovel full of snow, laughing as he dropped the snow directly into Otto's right ear. Dolph ran when Otto woke up with a start, his hand trying desperately to warm his ear back up again. Otto made his way to the bathroom to assess the situation. There didn't appear to be any frostbite, thank goodness, but his swollen ear glowed red from the bitter cold, melting snow falling out of his ear like a waterfall. "DOLPH!!" he yelled, "you will regret this!! You shall rue, Dolph, the red snow drained ear!!"

QUIT YOUR PINING

The annual Montgomery Flora Competition was the most prestigious event of it's kind. Gardeners from around the world gathered to parade the efforts of their work in a variety of categories, hoping for the coveted Montgomery Medal of Excellence. One entry, however, seemed a little out of place. The judges were perplexed. It didn't seem to fit in any award category and was simply unlike anything they had ever seen before. "Pardon me, young lady – just what on earth is this?" one judge asked Ivy, a gardener from Alberta. "Let me tell you," she began, "it took me forever to grow this, let alone find it. This, ladies and gentlemen, is a cottonwood. Not just any cottonwood – this is just one of only seven throughout the world. I climbed dozens of mountains in North America looking for it, and it was blind luck that I found it at all." The judges huddled together – it was a magnificent find, and the effort alone was impressive. But, rules were rules. The judges broke apart, and the head judge walked over to Ivy. "So amazing, miss, but unfortunately, this is a competition for standard flora, not a poplar rarity contest."

SEVENTH INNING EXTINCTION

The group of paleontologists were almost in disbelief. If they hadn't seen it in front of their eyes, they would have laughed at the very idea. Yet here it was, unearthed after millions of years – a broad field that looked very much like a baseball diamond, riddled with dinosaur fossils and what appeared to be some sort of a scoreboard. Gingerly they walked across the field, careful to avoid disturbing the frail finds of the excavation. A small number of them approached the pseudo scoreboard and dusted it off. There were markings – a line straight down the middle and scratches that looked strangely similar to counting. Affixed on top of one side was a small dinosaur tooth, while a patch of hair was at the top of the other. "It looks like they were playing a game," the head of the group said. "A baseball-type game. And they were keeping score – on a guess I'd assume it was dinosaurs versus mammals. What's most interesting, though," he continued, "count them up. On the mammal side, there are seven marks. On the dinosaur side, only six." "Doesn't look like it would have been that way for long," a voice bellowed from the home plate area, "look, this creature here looks like it was sliding into home plate, about to even the score. Judging by the size I'd say it's a Tie-run-asaurus Rex."

DEFINITELY PAST ITS PRIMATE

It was upsetting for the zookeeper. Sparky, an ape that had endeared itself to the zoo staff and the public, was acting very oddly of late. He would sit off to the corner, only looking up now and again if one of the keepers walked over. He refused to eat or drink. The vet had ruled out any sickness, though, and chalked it up to Sparky being lonely and depressed. He hated to see his simian friend in such distress. The zookeeper tried everything – singing, dancing, treats – but nothing seemed to cheer Sparky up. As the zookeeper was pondering what he could try next, he happened upon a garage sale. In a box was a large number of Raggedy Ann dolls being sold for ten cents each. Inspired, the zookeeper bought the entire box and brought it back to the zoo. Picking one of the dolls out of the box, he took it into Sparky's room and held it out for Sparky to see. Immediately, Sparky perked up and walked over. Taking the doll, he threw it up, caught it, and brought it to his chest for a long, warm hug. A smile crossed Sparky's lips as he took the doll over to his food and water, where he ate and drank for the first time in days. Days went by. Sparky and the Raggedy Ann doll were inseparable. The zookeeper was thrilled and pondered why this strategy was working while nothing else seemed to. "I guess it's true what they say," the zookeeper thought to himself, "dime Anns are a gorilla's best friend."

THE AWARD FOR BEST SUPPORTING SALAD GOES TO...

The critics all agreed – Nat's performance in the movie was by far the best of the year. There was even talk that Nat could win the Oscar for Best Actor. The film was pretty standard, a young cabbage seeking vengeance on the vegetables that kept him away from the dinner table. But Nat, starring as Cole the cabbage in the movie, owned the part like no other actor ever could have. As a result, millions of dollars came in from those that ran to see "Cole's Law."

LIVE AND LET VIPER

The county had the largest number of snake bites per capita in the country. As a result, it also held the highest rate of death by snake. The number of instances was so high that it prompted the opening of a funeral parlor devoted exclusively to those that died by venomous bites. It proved to be of great comfort to the family and friends of those that had perished, offering services, and support unique to their tragic circumstance. People had nothing but good things to say about the parlor, "Hiss and Hearse."

HOBOKEN OR BUST

"Well now, isn't this interesting," the art critic began, "so life-like, so creative, so avant-garde..." The curator of the museum smiled as he said, "yes, we are quite taken with this exhibit ourselves." The busts were indeed unique – each one made to look like a beggar, each one fashioned using newspaper and glue. The critic continued, "and these will be available for the public to see... when?" "Next week," the curator replied, "we've already been advertising and have an area on the second floor ready for these to be added." "Well, color me impressed!" the critic exclaimed. The curator smiled again – this was very high praise for a pauper mache exhibit.

LOOKS LIKE A STAFF INFECTION

The CEO looked sternly at the HR director across the table from him. With a heavy sigh, he began to speak. "So let me get this straight. You were asked to hire twenty people for the company. You did that, but each one is either a direct relation to you or is a friend of yours. Did you not think at any time that that may not be the best course of action?" The HR director gulped and responded directly to the question. "Sir, if I may," she began, "I was simply told to hire twenty people. I was not given any guidance as to what qualifications to hire for, what departments the positions were in, not even a list of previous experiences that would be of use. As a result, I turned to the people I knew best and hired them." The CEO pondered, "so what you're saying is you were just given the number of positions available to be filled?" "Correct," she replied, "it became a matter of personnel preference."

THE PLASTIC OH-NO BAND

The paper was perfect – after hours and hours of typing, lab research, compilations of data, and more, Stu finally had something he could present to the university. He ran a spell-check to ensure that nothing would distract from his ground-breaking work. Satisfied, Stu saved his document and sent the file to the printer for the required hard copy of the paper. However, as he looked at the paper, he was stunned to see that each and every space between words now had punctuation. Frantic, he ran back to his laptop and looked. Sure enough, there on the screen was the soft copy of his paper, littered with punctuation marks. Stu looked around and saw his fatal flaw – he thought he had turned the auto-punctuation feature off, but it had remained active. "Dammit," Stu thought, "instant comma's gonna get you, every time."

COME VALHALLA OR HIGH WATER

"Sir, you've got to hear this," the young communications officer beckoned. The captain walked over, knelt, and listened. It was faint, but you could still make out the words – Thor Thor Thor, Odin Odin Odin, Thor Thor Thor – over and over again. Immediately the captain sprang up and barked orders. "All personnel to your stations! We are on a rescue mission, effective immediately!" The officer looked perplexed. "Pardon, sir," he asked the captain, "but I don't understand – what does the message mean?" "Quite simply, son," he replied, "it's an urgent call for help, using Norse code."

MEAT AND GREET

Jim was thrilled. Chelsea, his girlfriend of 3 months, had just won the 2019 Alberta Beef beauty pageant. Joy filled his heart as he saw the silver tiara and an abundant bouquet of roses handed to Chelsea, who was tearfully grateful for the win. He couldn't wait to see her, so he ventured his way to the backstage area and was about to go in when a security guard stopped him. "I'm sorry – you are not allowed in," the guard said gruffly. "But my girlfriend just won," Jim explained, "I want to go backstage and congratulate her." The guard sighed, lifted his hand, and pointed to the large sign that read "FAMILY ONLY ALLOWED BACKSTAGE" and said, "you must be Miss Steak kin."

BUTT THEN AGAIN...

"Good work, everyone, good work," Bruce, the gym instructor, stated to his class as he reached for his water. He was popular among the gym members. Bruce was always encouraging, always rotated his class routines to work on the whole body, and was keenly aware of the latest workout regimes and their effectiveness. Today the talk around the gym was that Bruce had been studying routines to help strengthen hindquarters. Sure enough, after a quick swig of water, Bruce turned his attention back to the class and said, "Okay, now we're going to start working on our buttocks – they often get overlooked when doing exercises, so typically are not as strong as they could be." Bruce turned around, bent over, and began, "so follow me – rears out and start moving those rumps up and down, side to side." One class member put up her hand and asked, "does this actually work?" Bruce chuckled and replied, "absolutely, it's the latest trend. Everybody's twerking for the weak end."

"OH, HELLO, MR. TYLER – CHOWING... DOWN?"

The hotel manager sighed. He had taken a call from Aerosmith's tour manager. They were coming to town at the end of the month, so she needed to book rooms for the band. She had also listed several necessary items and steps that they would require during their stay. Most of them were pretty standard – keep water bottles cold and on hand, one flat of Budweiser per day, Hershey Kisses in a pink bowl – but it was one demand, in particular, that was troublesome. The band's primary demand for food was sandwiches at breakfast, lunch and dinner. Even snacks had to be sandwiches. That in itself wasn't so odd, but they specifically requested that the bread for their sandwiches be stored in the lift. "So daft," the manager thought to himself, "who prefers to have loaf in an elevator?"

THE VERY NEXT DAY
AND JUST WOULDN'T GO AWAY

Infuriated, Henry threw his smartphone across the room. After a few moments to calm down, he walked over and picked it up again. "I swear to God if it does it again this time…" he muttered as he began typing. It looked promising this time – the email he was composing wasn't showing anything odd – but just when he was about to hit "Send," it happened again. For weeks now, and despite numerous calls to support lines and Google website visits on how to fix it, his email address changed from henry123@hotmail.com to henry123-kitten-hotmail.com. Henry stared at the phone, his mouth agape, before exclaiming, "I can't believe it. I seriously can't believe it. I can't believe the cat in the @ came back."

JUST SINGING IN THE GRAIN

Jim's car, somehow, managed to sputter off to the side of the road before dying on him. "Great, just great," he said as he exited the vehicle, slamming the door forcefully behind him. He took in the surroundings – it was a back road in a rural farming community, and Jim had ended up by a large grain field. He pulled out his phone. Luckily, the reception was pretty decent, so Jim was able to get hold of a tow truck. As he waited from the field, he could hear what sounded like singing, followed by a chop. "Do, re, mi… CHOP. Do, re, mi… CHOP," over and over again. His curiosity getting the better of him, Jim walked through the field to the source of the sound. What he found was an elderly farmer, scythe in hand, singing and chopping the grain in a fluid motion. "Excuse me," Jim interrupted, "I'm sorry to bother you, but my car stalled on me just over here, and I couldn't help but hear you. May I ask what you're doing?" The farmer placed his scythe down, wiped the sweat from his brow, and began to speak. "My papa was a farmer on this here piece of land," the farmer explained, "and when I was growing up, he taught me all there was to know about farmin'. Whatever he did, he would have me do in the same manner. I learned milkin' cows, baling hay, collectin' eggs from the chickens, and this." The farmer stopped briefly to look up, and continued, "I followed him out here one day. He had this very scythe in his hand, and he would sing three notes and then swipe at the grain. Then he gave me the scythe and said, "alright, son, here's what you do. You don't reap after do, you don't reap after re, but I do need you to reap wheat after mi."

MAY THE FOURS BE WITH YOU

George couldn't sleep. It was the same uneasiness that had been plaguing him for days, keeping him from slumber. He tried to figure out what exactly it was that was bothering him but to no avail. George would remember seeing visions of a boat on the water suddenly capsize, but the images came and went so quickly he constantly felt edgy. Finally, the morning came. He wearily put on his clothes and waited downstairs for his friend Bill. When Bill came to the door, he excitedly said, "Dude! I rented a large canoe. Sid and Aidan are gonna come too – maybe we can get some fishing in or something!" Suddenly George knew what was happening. "NO!! We can't do that!" he yelled, shaking Bill viciously, "we could die!!" Bill, taken aback from the reaction, shyly asked, "what?" "It's true," George replied, allowing himself to calm down, "I've been troubled all week. I didn't understand until now – it was a sense of four boating."

RITE ON, MAN - THAT'S SO GROOVY

Father Jensen, the local Catholic prison chaplain, smiled as he looked out upon the chapel. Each pew was filled with repentant prisoners. And for a good reason — Father Jensen had worked long and hard in developing a sacred ritual that would absolve prisoners of their guilt, allowing them to be set free. And to his credit, Father Jensen knew that it couldn't be the long, drawn-out, tedious ritual that was sanctioned by the church. To encourage the prisoners to come, he had to revise the service so that it became more contemporary, more interesting, and infinitely cooler. Now here it was, December 24th, and the result of his hard work and planning was about to begin. As he walked to the front of the altar, Father Jensen recalled the people that supported his initiative, but he also remembered those that opposed and discredited it. He remembered vividly the day he pitched his idea to the justice board. Most were hesitant but were won over by his passionate speech, the one where he boldly proclaimed that he wanted to do his hip old pardon mass for Christmas, and only a hip old pardon mass would do.

BREAKFAST IS A BUCK

Juan loved venison. Ever since he was a child, he couldn't get enough of it. He had venison bacon, venison burgers, venison lunch meats, venison desserts – Juan even had a regular shipment of venison cereal, Bambi-Os, sent to his home. And not just small portions either – he would gorge himself on venison regularly. Alas, as the years went by, Juan's health deteriorated, and at the ripe old age of 95 he passed away. At his memorial, the pastor said to the gathered, "Juan was a good man, a just man, and lord how he loved venison. It was a Juan deer full life."

WOULD WE CALL IT BETTER FRIDAY?

John thought the idea was brilliant. Being a passionate Christian, he wanted to ensure that as many people as possible revered the entire Easter season. He also knew that for reasons beyond their control, some people missed out on the whole 40 days. And that was when the idea struck. Why not have a second Lenten season, one right after the first, so more people could participate? So here he was, standing before the collected heads of the city's religious community, pitching his idea. Once John had clearly explained his proposal, he left the room to allow for the group to talk it over. While he couldn't hear what was said, he did know that the discussion was very lively. Finally, the door opened, and he was invited back in. He sat down to await their decision. And they had decided alright – not only did they think it was a horrible idea but every member expressed their malcontent in a verbal barrage. As they left, John was left behind to ponder what had happened. He still liked the idea, but they obviously did not. They were re-Lent less.

... AND ON SALE FOR ONLY ONE HENRY THE VIIIth OF MANUFACTURER'S RETAIL PRICE

The Johnson's were torn. Their old car had only barely made it to the car lot, giving up the ghost as they pulled into the visitor parking stall. They were shopping for a new vehicle regardless, but this gave the purchase a degree of urgency. Despite their obvious need, the salesperson, Jill, had been very gracious about not taking unfair advantage of the situation and patiently listened to them. Having written everything down, Jill turned to her laptop and brought up the inventory list. After filtering on several criteria, she narrowed the choices down to three vehicles. There was a red Volkswagen Beetle, a Chevrolet Impala, and a car of unknown origin that had a picture of Queen Elizabeth I in the window and a certificate of authenticity that indicated it had belonged to an old royal house of Welsh origin. All three had their pros and cons, and the Johnson's marveled at how each handled their test drives. After standing in the corner and discussing for a time, they walked over to Jill's office. "We've made our decision, Jill," Mr. Johnson stated, "We love all three, but we've decided we don't want the Beetle or the Impala. We'll go for the Tudor."

CAMP WAS TOTALLY DRAINING

"You're going to have to do better than that, son," the camp leader barked at Dylan, "you won't drain a damn thing at that rate." Dylan sighed and tried again. He had signed up for camp earlier in the year, intrigued by its promise of teaching how to prepare a meal under a teepee. What Dylan hadn't expected was how difficult the tasks would become. That said, he had managed to do very well up until today's session – how to use a colander in a teepee. It sounded like it should be easy, but it ended up being very in-tent sieve training.

WORMS FOR LUNCH? I'M HOOKED

Arthur could barely stand the pain as he sat in the emergency room. It was his fault, he knew, agreeing to eat an entire pail of worms in the fishing shop on a double-dare from his buddies. He did admit that they acted quickly when the stomach pains started, getting him to the hospital right away. They did many tests on Arthur, and he was just waiting for the doctor to come, give him the results, and what the next steps were. It seemed to take forever, and what made it worse was the constant burping and the aroma of worm that came with it. Finally, the doctor came in and asked, "are you ready to hear the results, Arthur?" Arthur gulped and replied, "yes, please – I've been waiting here with baited breath."

WHERE'S PASTOR WALDO?

The congregation was worried. The vicar had left last month on a good-will aid trip overseas. Initially, he had been giving regular updates on his activities. Over the previous week, though, they had heard nothing from him at all. His social media accounts hadn't been updated in some time either, so naturally, they were concerned and feared the worst. The deacon was appointed to begin a concentrated search for the vicar, so he started with the local police. He strolled into the local precinct and waited for his turn to speak to the sergeant on duty. When his turn came up, the deacon walked forward, sighed, and explained what was happening. The sergeant listened intently, taking a few notes here and there until the deacon had finished speaking. The sergeant reached for a form and said, "I'm sorry to hear about this, and I understand your concern. We'll initiate a search straight away, but I'm just going to need you to fill out this mission parsons report first."

COME OUT AND GAY

Beth scanned the entire room, looking for her friend Lee, to no avail. The place was crowded, to be fair, but she still was adamant that Lee had to be here. The party was for Lee, after all, in celebration of her courage to come out as a lesbian. Beth herself wasn't a lesbian but still appreciated just how hard it must have been for Lee to do and wanted to congratulate her face to face. It was proving impossible, however. She had no problem identifying a number of the people there, including their mutual friend Laraine who was hanging out by the punch bowl. Hoping that Laraine maybe had some insight, Beth started to walk towards the punch bowl herself. She was almost there when Laraine turned and headed the other way, and it was then that Beth saw Lee, who had been standing there the entire time behind Laraine. Beth lightened up and thought to herself, "ah, I can see queer Lee now. Laraine is gone."

DON'T YOU KNOW VIRACOCHA LOVES YOU

The thick layer of dust was a testament to just how long the videocassette had been locked away, but Henry finally had found it. The video was a proverbial unicorn, with many believing it to be just a myth, so the excitement Henry felt holding it in his hands was well earned. It was rumored to be the only copy in existence. It was a professionally edited copy of a staged Andrew Lloyd Webber musical as directed by I. Ron Butterfly that replaced and inserted the names of Incan deities throughout the dialogue and lyrics, that had only ever played once on Broadway. Henry gently placed the cassette into the VCR, smiling as the television crackled to the sound of "Don't Cry For Me Apocatequil." Picking up his phone, he called the museum curator right away. "Hey, it's Henry," he bellowed, "I've got it. It's legit. It's an Incan God dubbed Evita, baby!"

ROLLING OUT THE RED CARP

The aquarium was the focal point of the entire lobby. People would come in from off the street to marvel at just how exquisite it was, and how peaceful it was watching the large carp swimming around. What set it apart, though, was that each carp was a bold bluish-green color, an extreme rarity. It was so rare that a plaque, explaining where the fish originated, was made. It read, "Most large carp are bred in Japan and distributed worldwide. The carp you see in the aquarium here are not from Japan – they are actually bred in Ankara. That makes them Turk kois."

DID WE NOT LITERALLY JUST SEE ANOTHER MONARCHY JOKE?

It was 1533 BC in London, England, and walking through the streets and towards the palace was a young man carrying a large bag. The young man knocked on the castle door. As the large door opened, a servant stepped forward and asked, "how can I help you, sir?" The young man began speaking, "not how you can help me, but how I can help you – more specifically, how I can help the king. May I speak with him?" The servant, somewhat taken aback, replied, "you want to speak with King Henry the VIIIth? What on earth could you possibly want to speak to him regarding? His majesty is very busy, having just married Anne Boleyn over the weekend." The young man was adamant. "He needs to see me," he asserted, "I have the largest collection of luxury goods from France, with strict instructions to sell only to the royal family. I'm a Dior Tudor salesman."

THE HILLS ARE ALIVE... RUN! RUN FOR YOUR LIVES! THEY'RE COMING THIS WAY!!

The opening of the latest Broadway revival of "The Sound Of Music" was just a few weeks away, and as with any production, the set pieces were still under construction. A few had been completed, like the Von Trapp family home, and some were nearing completion. One of these was the mountain top set, and it was proving to be quite tricky. It was large, bulky, and for some reason, there were several places where the interior framework refused to stay together. "I dunno, Jim," Ralph said from underneath the piece, "I can't get these boards to stay together down here. I've tried nails, screws..." "Stop there. I know what you need," Jim offered. He stepped away for a few minutes, and when he returned, Jim had a couple of items in his hands. "Here," he said to Ralph as he passed the pieces down, "try these." Ralph

looked and shook his head. "Glue? I've already tried glue," he said in frustration, "it doesn't work." "It

will now," Jim replied, "glue the pieces and hold them together with the Edelweiss grip."

WELL, ITS BEEN A SLICE

Ed sighed. He knew this day was coming, he knew it was coming when he committed his heinous crimes, and finally, it was here. Capital punishment by guillotine, although rare in the state, was still an option in the sentencing of the worst of the worst, and Ed was the very definition of that. So in the hours leading up to his fate, he began to clean up his cell. He had swept the floor, made the bed, and was just about to organize the collection of books when the warden arrived. "You ready, Ed?" the warden asked. "Not quite," Ed replied, "I've just got a few more things to do in here, and then I'll head off."

CAN YOU DIG IT? AGAIN?

King Harold had gathered his aides together. "Gentlemen," he began, "I've noticed that the moat around the castle here is, well, it's in terrible shape." With that, he motioned for the aides to go to the window and look. Sure enough, the trench looked awful. The water was turning into a sickly shade of green, the retaining walls were crumbling apart, and the smell was unpleasant at best. Once they had returned to the table, King Harold resumed. "I need ideas," he stated, "we can't let this go on, so any suggestions?" The aides talked amongst themselves and began pitching ideas. "We could just fill it in with cement." "We could sell the green water as a vegetable-based beverage?" "Just fix it?" These were just a few ideas, but the king wasn't fond of any of them. Finally, one aide raised his hand and said, "well, what if we did fill this one in, but dug a second trench around the castle and filled it with water?" The king pondered. "I like it. I don't love it, but I like it," he said, "it's definitely a re-moat possibility."

SURVIVOR OF THE FITTEST

Lady Helena felt nauseous. Having been kidnapped by pirates certainly didn't help, but the sea itself was violently rocky. Finally, feeling a touch better, she opened the door and stepped out onto the deck. It was there she looked up and saw the ruthless pirate Tealbeard at the wheel, shouting at a nearby dog. She moved closer – she was not intimidated by Tealbeard and was curious about what he was yelling at the dog. Finally, Lady Helena was close enough to hear, and she could barely believe it. Tealbeard, the fearsome pirate, was asking the dog which way he should turn to storm the sea, and the dog would bark once or twice depending upon the query. Despite the ship bobbing dangerously, she giggled at the madness of what she was hearing, catching the attention of Tealbeard. "My lady Helena," he began, "what be so funny?" "My apologies, captain," she replied, "but why on earth are you asking directions from this pet?" Tealbeard smiled slightly. Even he knew how silly the sight must be to outsiders, but he answered. "This is Scurvy, a mongrel I picked up in Thailand," Tealbeard said, "and he has a rare and precious gift. He knows which way to turn the ship for the safest navigation." A wave hit the front of the ship at that moment, so Tealbeard cut short his tale to Lady Helena and asked Scurvy, "should I turn to starboard, Scurvy?" Scurvy let out a single, loud bark, prompting the pirate to turn to port. "That's amazing," she uttered, "so one bark means no, I take it?" "Correct," he replied, "one bark is nay." He then asked Scurvy if he should turn to starboard now, at which the dog barked twice. "And when he barks twice, that is not a nay," he continued, "that is the aye of the Thai cur."

SURVIVOR OF THE FITTEST II - IT DOESN'T GET ANY BETTER

Lady Helena was not a big fan of flying, but it was the only way to get to the reception in Switzerland on time. So she put on her bravest face and marched up the stairs and into the plane. Thankfully, the take-off was uneventful, and the ride smooth, so Helena was feeling much less anxious than she had before. She even took a look out of the window once in a while. It was during one of these looks that something caught her eye. There, draped vertically over a mountain in the Swiss Alps, was a long, large piece of fabric. "Pardon me, Sven," Lady Helena asked the Swiss attendant, "but what is that piece of fabric doing on that mountain?" Sven bowed gently and replied, "Lady Helena, today is National Formal Mountain Day in Switzerland. We dress up the mountains in formal attire every year. What you see there is the tie. The tie of the Eiger."

SURVIVOR OF THE FITTEST III - KIDDING! JUST BRING IT BACK WHEN YOU'RE DONE

"I know it's a strange request," the Canadian Prime Minister began, "but Canada is uneven right now, and we could really use the help." The President of the United States pondered. It was indeed a strange request, asking to borrow one of the 50 states to create balance in Canada. Yet he knew how often Canada had been an ally, and he did have 50 states after all. "Alright," the President replied as he pointed to the upper north-west corner on the map, "you can have this one." The PM was ecstatic. "Thank you so much," he joyously proclaimed, "I really appreciate you being an Oregon donor."

WHERE'S MY SECRETARIAT?

Jess walked over to the magnificent beast. HER beast. Volt was older now but was still one handsome racehorse. As she gently stroked his mane, the owner of the local racetrack, Jim, came over. They had mutual respect for one another – Jess was a top-notch jockey, while Jim was one of the few honest track owners she had known, never one to put the riders or their horses in danger. As Jim came nearer, he began. "Jess, I have a problem, and I hope you can help," he said, pausing only briefly, "we have several races scheduled for this afternoon but are short on horses. Would you and Volt be able to come out?" Jess pondered briefly before answering, "he can run all out for a good minute, but not very far and definitely not furlong."

JUST GETTING UP TEEPEE

Dan Crowfeather was nervous. He had never entered a costume contest before, and to make things interesting his costume wasn't a typical pop culture icon. Dan's costume was a testament to his native heritage and his love of comic books. He had dressed up as a First Nations superhero. As he walked across the stage, he was encouraged by the positive response from the crowd. He stopped about halfway and waited for the judge's assessment. "Hello, Dan," one judge asked, "and you are dressed as a…". "Native superhero!" he said boldly. "Well, that's a ten, and good for your original design," the judge replied with a smile, "that's mighty brave."

LET'S SPEND THE NIGHT TO FEATHER

Sal hadn't been into work all week, and his supervisor Glenda was flustered. He had called in every day without fail, but his reason for not being at work sounded ludicrous. No one had ever come up with an excuse like having to keep an eagle's home warm before, but Sal had used it all week. It irked her to no end, so she finally decided to go and see Sal for herself. She arrived at his home, slammed the car door, and ran up. "Sal, Sal!" she yelled as she knocked loudly on the door, "It's Glenda. Where are you?" "Up here," a shout came from above. Glenda looked up, and sure enough, there was Sal, sitting in a giant bird home. "Oh, you really are keeping it warm," she said, "it just sounded so odd that I didn't believe you." Sal replied, "that's okay. I get it, but I was completely on nest."

I'LL JUST TAKE A TAXIDERMY HOME

Zack waited impatiently at the counter of the local taxidermist. "Are they almost ready?" he barked. He didn't mean to be so, but it was Halloween, and he needed his pieces for decorations before kids started showing up. "Yes, sir," came the reply, "right here." Zack was impressed. The small wolf and seagull were absolutely perfect. "If I may ask, sir," the taxidermist asked as he rang the sale through, "what are these for?" Zack handed over his credit card and said, "it's Halloween. I need to put out my jackal and tern."

FREEZE! OH, YOU ALREADY DID

A little known historical fact of interest - In the early days of the FBI agents were continually making breakthroughs in the field of crime-solving. DNA testing, dusting for fingerprints, reenacting crime scenes – these all came about as a result of their hard work. One of the most impressive, though, was their assessment of the size, location, and imminent danger of the iceberg that ultimately sank the Titanic before the event even happened. Hundreds would have been saved had they been listened to, but no one expected the success of glacial profiling.

I COULD REALLY GO FOR SOME JUJUJUJUBES

Pamela opened the hotel windows and breathed in the morning world of New Orleans. It was breathtaking, more beautiful, and grand than she had anticipated. It felt unlike any other city she had ever been to, and she loved being here. Wanting to take in as much as she could, Pamela threw on some clothes and stepped out into the street. She walked for a while, taking in the local shops and other sights when she came upon a large field of grass. Pamela thought she had seen something, or someone, so stopped to investigate. Sure enough, a man was lying down in the middle of the field, staring intently at the early morning moisture that had collected on the grass. Curious, she veered towards him and asked, "pardon me, sir – what are you doing?" The man gathered himself and stood up, his long tall frame towering over Pamela. "Shango is my name, my dear," he said politely, "and I was just practicing view dew."

MAYBE THE DINGO ATE YOUR LATTE

"Crikey, not again!" The angry cry reverberated through the Starbucks. Mike looked over to see a large Australian man, clearly frustrated at what Mike could only perceive was an incorrect order. Seeing the perplexed look on the barista's face, he walked over to see if he could help. "Hey, man, come with me," Mike said as he gently moved the man away from the counter and to a nearby chair. Mike took the opposite chair and introduced himself. "G' day. The name's Dundee," the Australian responded in kind, "I'm here from Sydney to visit some relatives." Seeing that his idea to remove Dundee from the situation had worked at calming him down, Mike asked, "what seems to be the problem, Dundee?" Dundee sighed and said, "I've asked this sheila for the same coffee order three times now, and it's been wrong each time. Each coffee has had a large amount of ashes stirred into it. It can't be that difficult, can it? It's simple – I just keep asking if I can have some cream, mate."

THANKS FOR CHAIRING

It was a slow news day, and the Channel 7 news copter was about to head back to the hangar when George saw a commotion below. In the hotel parking lot, it looked like a large group of people were swinging hotel chairs at one another. It was growing in intensity, but George couldn't be sure that's what he was seeing. "It can't be, can it?" George thought to himself as he strained his eyes to see. Positive that it was indeed a furniture brawl George pulled out the news camera and called out to the pilot, "swing low – suite chair riot."

HERE'S MY NUMBER - COLUMN ME MAYBE

It was a stupid argument to have, but an argument nonetheless. Quentin, Paul, and Alanis stood around the large column, and while standing there, the two men had a heated discussion about the style of the column. "It's Doric, Paul," Quentin shouted, "it's clearly Doric. Why is this even an issue for you?" "Because, you moron – it's Corinthian," Paul tallied, "anyone with the IQ of a rock can see that it's Corinthian!" The argument carried on this way for a solid 10 minutes, escalating in intensity. Each being completely unable to sway the other, they turned to Alanis and asked, "you know, Alanis. Doric or Corinthian?" Alanis looked up and down the column, touched the base, sighed, and said, "isn't it Ionic? Don't you think?"

JUST GO – I'LL TAKE THE WRAP

Bill put the fabric around his waist initially as a joke, but as he walked by the mirror, he paused. Looking at himself as if he were a Greek god, he thought, "holy crap, does this make me look amazing or what?" The salesclerk walked over, chuckling to herself at the sight of Bill turning and gazing at himself, and said, "it's from Indonesia, and I have to admit it looks terrific on you." "True that," Bill confessed, "I would never have thought a fabric wrap would make me look like this. How can something sarong be so right?"

SHUT YOUR FLAP, JACK

"You've made it to the prize round!" Sharon could barely hold her excitement. "Spam Aces" had been her favorite game show growing up, so to hear host Terry Jones say the magic words to her in person was a dream that had come true. "Okay, Sharon, here's the deal," Terry said, "you have to pick two out of these three choices." He motioned over to the left, where the curtain opened to reveal her options. Terry continued, "You can go out the door on the left, where you are guaranteed to win $200 and a flat of Spam. You can choose a year's supply of pancake mix, that may or may not contain cash up to $10,000. Or, you can choose to have this poet on the right create and read out a poem about you, and after the reading, you keep the poem, which may or may not contain cash up to $10,000. You'll then spin the Spam wheel to see which of the two choices you end up receiving. What do you choose, Sharon?" Sharon pondered. It was risky. The last two choices could net $10,000, but she'd seen enough shows where the contestant did not win any cash. The first choice was at least $200 guaranteed, and she could use it. Finally, Sharon sighed and said, "I'll go with options 2 and 3. Option 1 is tempting, but I'm gonna go for it – for batter or verse."

THE PLUMAGE DON'T ENTER INTO IT!

The animal control bylaw officer and the police constable sat side by side in the cruiser, each looking intensely at sidewalks, down alleys and storefronts as they drove down the street. "Anything?" the constable asked. "No, nothing yet," the bylaw officer responded. The sergeant had made it abundantly clear – priority number one was to track down the Peacock Gang. Each member was a large, gay game bird with extravagant plumage, and the city lived in fear of the many criminal activities that the birds had been committing recently. Just then, the radio crackled. It was the sergeant, asking for an update. "Nothing so far, sarge," the constable replied. "Keep looking," the sergeant commanded, "these birds represent a queer and pheasant danger."

HEAD AND SHOULDERS, SEEDS AND GROWS

"That'll do," the old farmer said as he passed the last bottle of shampoo to his son. They scanned across the field of grain, and it did indeed look like every square inch had been covered in shampoo and soaped up. As they walked back to the barn, the farmer said, "so we'll let that sit about 15 minutes before we get the big hose out and wash the shampoo out." His son nodded silently at first, but then a quizzical look came across his face, and he asked, "Dad, I've gotta know. Every year we do this routine, and I still don't understand why we can't collect the grain without shampooing and watering first. So, why?" The old farmer stopped in his tracks, smiled quietly, and replied, "it's the way that it's always been, boy. Lather, rinse, and reap wheat."

WE NEED TO TACO

Finally, the after-tremors stopped, and the team stepped out from their shelter. They had been sent to the geologic fracture to monitor it for seismic activity, yet none had been recorded for days. Today, however, Jimmy had walked over to the anomaly and kicked it, and almost immediately the earthquake began. Dusting himself off, Jimmy said to the rest of the team, "oh man... that's on me. That's my fault. It has to be, somehow. I'm so sorry..." Darlene, the leader of the team, stopped him there and said, "no, no, Jimmy. It's not you. Look over there. What do you see?" She had pointed to an area farther up the fracture, so Jimmy looked and said, "it looks like someone's dumped a huge amount of tortilla chips, cheese, sour cream, and guacamole into the crack." "Exactly," Darlene assured him, "that's what caused the earth's crust to shift here. It's nacho fault."

FANTASTIC LANDSCAPING ON A SHEEP BUDGET

The figurine had become the talking point of the town. Jerry had placed, in the town hall courtyard, a giant statue of a sheep crafted entirely out of cedar. It had taken him weeks to finish, but all who passed by were amazed by the intricate detail Jerry had gently placed on his work. The crazy thing was that no one had even asked Jerry to do it. Most had assumed that perhaps the mayor had commissioned the job, but he was just as lost as anyone else. Miles, the local newspaper reporter, tracked Jerry down and asked, "the sheep looks absolutely stunning, Jerry, but... well, why?" Jerry hesitated only briefly before he answered; "dunno – wooden ewe?"

I DID NAZI THAT COMING

"You have to take that off," the editor barked as he threw the paper layout on Eva's desk. Composing herself, she asked, "take what off?" The editor looked at her in disbelief. "What do you mean, take what off?" he snapped, "it should be obvious, especially to the people of Berlin!" She looked again at the layout. It had been her responsibility for the last year to lay out the front page of the Berlin Newsenhammer paper, and this was the first time that the editor hadn't liked her work. "I'm sorry, herr editor – I just don't see what's wrong." He sighed, pulled up a chair, and began his explanation. "Fraulein, here's my issue. This story here, the top one about that Lear jet forced to land because it was getting completely pummelled by frozen rain." "What about it?" Eva asked. Still in disbelief, he answered, "it's the headline, Eva, the headline. Even though it's true, you simply can't put "Hail Hit Lear."

DAT IS DALLAS THING YOU'LL HEAR

There was no reasonable explanation for the phenomena. Slowly but surely, inch by inch, the state of Texas was sinking underwater. Entire fields, towns, even cities that had thrived for years were now simply gone. It was such a unique situation that while most people were fleeing the state, scientists eager to see first-hand were flocking in. Dr. Smithers was one of those that wanted to get there before it was too late, so he booked his ticket and was packing a suitcase when his wife came in and said, "why, why are you going? It's dangerous – you could die. Why would you leave me, the kids, for this?" "Honey," Dr. Smithers said calmly, "it's a once-in-a-lifetime opportunity. Things like this just don't happen in my field." His wife took it in, and with a stern look upon her face, stated, "if that's the way it's going to be, fine. If you stay, we carry on, but if you leave, you are not welcome back. Go to Texas if you want, but if you go, there's no Luckenbach."

TRANSPORTATION IS MY #1 PRIORITY - AND #2

Henry walked through the salesroom floor, eyeing up each ATV. He'd waited for years to get one and was now in the position he could. So Henry would look at the price tag, sit on an ATV, check things out and move on to the next. As he was doing so, there was one in the back corner that intrigued him. He walked over to assess it. The price was certainly reasonable, but to say it was odd-looking would be kind. The wheels were angled, the body was curved, and it came with a retractable face-mask. As he was looking, a salesperson walked over. "Can I help you, sir?" she asked. "Perhaps," Henry replied, "what is the deal with this ATV?" She laughed and said, "ah, yes. It's a strange-looking beast, isn't it? It was designed for the sole purpose of traveling through large waste pipes. It's a sewer size quad."

MUST BE IN-BREAD

Farley went to the local sandwich shop, world-renowned for its use of fish in their wares. He scanned the menu – there was halibut and lettuce, hot squid and kale, cod and pickle sandwiches, the usual. But then he came across the special of the day – a Lion King sandwich. Farley asked the cashier about it, and she replied, "oh yes, the Lion King sandwich. That's hot tuna tomato." He ordered one to stay, picked it up, and walked towards the dining area. As he rounded the corner, Farley saw there were napkins all over the floor. He pointed it out to one of the staff, who stressed that not moments ago they were all together on the counter. "Ah," he said, "so it's the fall of the former serviette union." "But it happened so fast!" "Of course," Farley said, "They're rushin…"

JUST SIT BACK AND STAIR

The Finsters went away for the weekend only to come back and see that their basement, which was only partially developed when they left, was now finished. They hadn't hired anyone, nor did it appear that anyone had even been in the house. But as Mr. Finster walked around the basement, he found several empty beer bottles along the wall. He sighed and confronted the basement. "Got drunk, did we basement?" he accused. The basement denied vehemently, saying it didn't drink at all. Mr. Finster said, "I don't believe it... look at you. You're plastered." The basement still denied any wrongdoing, saying the finishing wasn't its fault. It had, in fact, been framed.

FEELING UNDER PRESSURE - 30 PSI, IN FACT

Bart simply wasn't feeling himself. He couldn't quite place what was wrong, but he just knew it was something. He managed to get himself to his doctor's office and waited patiently for the doctor's arrival. As the doctor came in, he asked Bart, "what seems to be the trouble, young man?" "I don't know," Bart started, "I just feel off. It feels like handlebars are growing out of my head, pedals out of my hips, a chain in my arm…" The doctor stopped him there and said, "you feel like a bicycle." "That's it!" Bart exclaimed, "that's exactly it. Why?" The doctor looked at him and said, "you need sleep. You're two tired." Bart shook his head and said, "no, no, it's worse than that, I think – I feel like a bicycle, but only on its rear tire." The doctor replied, "then you desperately need some sleep. You're wheelie tired."

NICE DAY TO GO FOR A SQUAWK

Nancy had shown up at the zoo for her job interview. The zoo was looking for someone to restock their bird exhibits regularly, and with her passion for birds, it would be a perfect fit. The HR head brought her into his office and began. "What we are looking for, Nancy, is someone to maintain the bird exhibits and ensure that new birds are rotated in regularly." "I'm precisely who you need, sir," Nancy said. The HR head chuckled and said, "I love that enthusiasm! You are hired." Nancy was a little taken aback at how successful this interview had been but replied, "oh, thank you! You won't regret it." He answered back, "I suspect I won't regret it at all. So what the job entails is bringing in swallows every month, owls brought in semi-monthly, and flamingos every three months." "Sounds good," Nancy said as she wrote the information down, "now what about the Birds of Prey exhibit? How often is that turned around?" "The Birds of Prey?" he answered, "purely on an add-hawk basis."

ALL YOU NEED IS LOVE – AND MAYBE A SPLASH OF COLOR ON THAT WALL...

Fun fact – Ronald Wrigley of Liverpool has the only home in the world that is decorated exclusively in a Beatles theme. The exterior is painted to look like the "Sgt. Pepper" album cover, the furniture is crafted to look like items from "Yellow Submarine," and the doorbell chimes "Day Tripper" when pressed. The living room windows are covered in Paul drapes. There are Ringo tablecloths in the dining room and George bedsheets in the guest room. And of course, the bathroom is stocked with John linen.

THAT ONE WENT RIGHT BAYOU

Interesting news out of Louisiana. In an effort to raise funds, the state department there has implemented a new fiscal strategy. New boat paddles sold within the state will not be released to the purchaser until that purchaser has cleared all outstanding debts. This includes back taxes, parking tickets, fines, and so on. So if you go to Louisiana to buy boating equipment, you can expect to see new oar liens.

TALK ABOUT TAKING A TIME OUT

Jeff went in to see the doctor. He was positive he wasn't crazy, but he wanted a medical opinion. After a few minutes, he was called into a back room, where the doctor followed shortly after. "So what seems to be the trouble, young man?" the doctor queried. Jeff looked around, as if to make sure there was no one there to hear him, and answered, "it sounds insane, I know, but I swear to you – I can make time stand still. Not for long, a few seconds, but definitely can. Have you ever heard of this before? Can this actually happen?" The doctor, unfazed by the oddity of Jeff's confession, said, "believe it or not, I have heard and seen this before. While I would prefer to say it's nonsense, it's definitely a pause ability."

I'LL HAVE NUNAVUT

The trinket caught Jim's eye. It was unlike anything he had seen before – handcrafted, clearly of an indigenous nature, and a color he could only describe as ice-blue. "Hey, honey," Jim said as he walked towards his wife Jan, "take a look at this. It's fascinating. Where do you think it's from?" Jan held it, looked it over, and said, "it's a carved figurine from an indigenous tribe in far northern Canada." "Really? How do you know?" Jim inquired. "Easy," Jan replied, "women's Inuition."

IT'S A TIC TAC, PADDY WHACK

I look back at my high-school years fondly. The friends that were by my side. The teachers whose efforts instilled a passion for learning. I remember heading to the library, finding a quiet corner, and working on the essay that was due in the next class. My locker, filled to the brim with schoolbooks, gym wear, and Coca-Cola. I remember the awards case that carried the honors of school sports teams throughout the ages. I remember when the principal unveiled the gift from the local candy factory, two large Tic-Tacs that each weighed precisely 28.35 grams. The pride in knowing we were the only school in the city that was entrusted with these unique items, and the great feeling of loss throughout the school when an errant water pipe dissolved the Tic Tacs overnight. Yes, I clearly remember the school mourning an ounce mints.

I CAN'T STAY, JUST POPPIN IN

"I'm sorry, can you tell me again?" Greg asked groggily. "Dude, you were sooooo drunk last night!" Bob replied, "I'm not surprised you can't remember much of it!" And Greg couldn't. Yesterday was his birthday, so he and his friends went out to the local club to celebrate. He remembered about the first hour of the night and then… bits and pieces at best, and Bob was only too happy to bring him up to speed. "So check the outgoing calls on your phone," Bob laughed. Greg brought his phone up, blinked a few times, and looked at his call history. "K. Frog? Like, Kermit the frog?" Greg asked. "Totally," Bob said, "you somehow got his number, called him up, and kept calling him a moron. Or dumbass. I think "twit" even came up. It didn't matter what Kermit said you would just reply "whatever, s-m-r-t guy. Whatever." It was hysterical!" "Okay, okay, I'll take your word on it," Greg said, "So what else happened?" Bob chuckled more and said, "You know Al, the bartender, right? He served us all night, was fantastic, so when the night was over we left a sizeable tip. You, however, insisted it was too much, pocketed most of it, and threw two bucks on the table." "Bloody hell," Greg said as he shook his head, "I can't believe I stupor called the frog a dipstick, next paid Al atrocious."

AT THE COUNT OF TWO, PRO-SEED

Bill walked the aisles of the farming equipment store. It was harvesting season, and although he didn't have a large farm, it was enough to support himself and his family. However, his harvest equipment was no longer up to the task. It needed replacement and time was short. "Can I help you, sir?" the young sales associate asked. "Yes, please," Bill replied, "I need some new tools to reap my wheat this year." "Follow me," she said as she led Bill down the aisle, "right here on your left." Bill was impressed. There was a large assortment of tools, and the prices were quite reasonable. Then off to the left, a tool caught his eye – it had a long, curved blade for reaping wheat but had two handles. "What is that?" Bill queried. "That, sir, is a new product this year. It allows for multiple people to do the reaping," she explained, "it's a bi-sickle, built for two."

ITS FINGER-LICKIN'... WAIT, NO... ITS DINNER FORK AND KNIFE PLEASANT

"My God, this is absolutely delicious!" Kevin exclaimed, "never have I had such wonderful fried chicken!" Kevin called the waiter over and asked, "may I see the chef? This is the most amazing chicken I have ever had – I would love to know his secret!" The waiter looked nervous and said, "um... okay, but I will warn you that he doesn't really like people coming into his kitchen." Keith guffawed and said, "I don't care. I've gotta know." The waiter resigned himself and said, "very well, follow me." He led Keith to the back and called out, "Chef Carl, I have someone here who would like to talk to you." He then mumbled something quietly and retreated into the main dining area. Keith took a few steps in and looked around the corner. There he saw the strangest thing. Around the deep fryer was a string quartet playing Brahms, a butler that was escorting the prepared chicken to the basket, and a candelabra that hung from above, illuminating the entire area. "Who are you?!?" a cry came from behind Keith. He turned around to see the chef, dressed in a tuxedo and seething mad at the sight of him. "You must be Chef Carl," Keith said, "I am so sorry to intrude, but I simply had to tell you how wonderful your fried chicken is, and if I could have the recipe." Chef Carl looked at Keith, scowled even deeper, and said, "no, no, I will not do that. It's classy fried."

I WRITE THE SONGS ON DE-MANDY

There is exciting news in the world of archaeology and Biblical research. After months and months of excavations and research, it has been discovered that the legendary "Copacabana" night club is built upon holy land. Specifically, fossilized bread has been found, leading to the discovery that this was where the Lord dropped bread from the heavens for the Israelites. At first, they didn't understand why they had to dig so far down to find it. Upon further investigation, they found the answer was in the Bible all along. From Exodus, "the Lord dropped bread and said to the Israelites, "do not eat this first bread, but instead plant it so you may be fruitful." "How deep, Lord?" Moses asked. "Well," the Lord replied, "you must bury manna low."

I CAN'T DIVA-LGE THAT INFORMATION

The opera benefit wrapped up, clocking in at just over 2 hours, and all attendees were overjoyed at the experience. That is, all but Fulder. He sat in his seat, looking at the program, and shook his head. "There's something not right, Sully," he said to his wife, "look, here. It says that there would be just over 50 solos performed during the opera tonight, but I counted. And I only counted 50." "You're delusional," his wife countered, "there had to be over 50." "No, no," Fulder argued, "EXACTLY 50. There's a conspiracy going on, I know it. Follow me." He took Sully by the hand and walked toward the stage where a large security guard met them. "Pardon, sir, but maybe you know," Fulder inquired, "why were there only 50 solos when we were promised just over that?" "There was another solo," the guard replied, "but you didn't hear it. It was highly classified, and for your safety, it never existed at all." The pair were taken aback at the response. "So, there was over 50? Why can't we hear it?" Fulder asked. "Again, sir – it's highly classified, and even it's existence is not to be mentioned. We call it Aria 51."

WHEN IRISH EYES ARE SMILING, BUT EVERYTHING ELSE IS JUST FALLING OFF

The constable reached for his ringing phone. "Constable O'Reilly here," he answered, "how can I help you?" From the other end came the small, aged voice of an elderly lady." "Oh, constable," she began, "I think I may have been tricked into giving some money away." O'Reilly paused and sighed. It was the tenth call this morning, St. Patrick's Day no less, and all about the same thing, but he still had to ask. "I'm sorry m'dear," he said gently, "that's awful. May I ask what happened?" The lady started into her story. "Some young men came to the door, claiming that they had a severe skin disease and were asking for donations to find a cure. I gave them $100 and closed the door, only to see them run down the street laughing." O'Reilly wrote the information down and compared it to the accounts he had already heard. He then turned back to the phone and asked, "were the lads dressed in green, perhaps?" The old lady was surprised and said, "why, yes. Yes, they were. How did you know?" The constable answered back, "well, love – we've had many phone calls about the same group of boys. We've just been instructing people to look out for leper cons."

NOT SURE HOW THAT HAPPENED - I'M STUMPED

"Okay, hold the Oscar up and look over here," the photographer said. Rudy did as he was asked, smiling from ear to ear as he held up the award. It was a dream come true. Rudy never imagined that his documentary work would one day get him the Academy Award, but it did, and it felt amazing. After the hail of photographs were taken, Rudy was ushered into the interview room. "Excuse me, Rudy," one reporter asked, "you looked stunned that your name was called as the winner for a short-form documentary. Care to discuss?" Rudy chuckled and replied, "certainly. I absolutely was stunned – your instincts are correct. When I first started filming 'Marathon Gone,' it was just a story I felt needed telling, the story of Nigel Stumpins, a marathon runner whose legs simply fell off just a few steps into the 1987 Boston Marathon. And honestly, I didn't think anyone had ever seen it. It was released into theatres but didn't have a long run."

SEEING THINGS ISN'T ALL ITS CRACK UP TO BE

Jen was not feeling 100%, so went to the clinic, and was a little surprised that the doctor on call there was blind. She asked him if it was difficult being blind in his profession, to which he replied, "it's challenging, of course, but for any reports that come in that aren't in braille, or email, I do have a set of eyes on my butt I can use for reading." She found that fascinating but had no intention of confirming his statement. Anyways, they conducted a battery of tests on her, and a few minutes later, the doctor came back, a report in hand, and said, "your tests have come back, so if you'll excuse me a moment, I need to anal eyes these results."

SHE'S NOT UNUSUAL –SHE'S STARK RAVEN MAD. A POOCH WITH CAUTION

The renowned animal scientist addressed the members of the zoological society with her findings. "What we've discovered," she started, "is that different birds all have one strong, primary trait that defines what they do. For example, an eagle's primary trait is keeping consistent. A wren's primary trait is seeking shelter. A pigeon's primary trait is finding food." A hand popped up from the audience. "Yes, you have a question?" she asked. "I do," a man answered, "what about seagulls? From what I've seen, they don't seem to have one." "Wonderful question," she replied, "seagulls did present us with some challenges, but we eventually concluded that gulls just wanna have fun." The scientist paused and then continued with her speech. "Another interesting item we've discovered is that canines have a preferred media for playing music. Collies prefer iTunes, poodles like CDs, sheepdogs will only listen to LPs, terriers like cassettes and dalmatians, obviously, prefer Spotify."

YOU ARE SENTENCED FOR MURDER. TENOR TWENTY YEARS

The body lay there on the opera stage. The police showed up to investigate but were held up by the stage manager. "Excuse us," the officer said to the manager, "we need to do a proper assessment of the murder." "I understand, I do," the manager replied quietly, "but it's Lady Gertrude, the famous diva and the lead singer in the opera here. She has insisted upon continuing her solo without interruption." The officer and the investigative team sighed in unison. "Well," the officer said as he pointed to the singer, "we really don't care what she wants to do. We're going to need you to clear the aria."

TRANSIT... TRANSTAY... TRANROLLOVER... GOOD GIRL!

"Excuse me, ma'am," the bus driver said as he turned to talk to an elderly woman sitting at the front. "How can I help you, young man?" she replied. "This is somewhat awkward," the driver stammered quietly, "but I couldn't help but notice that you didn't pay the transit fee." "I most certainly did!" she roared back in defiance, "right there in the box. See?" The driver was surprised at the ferocity of the response but calmly looked in the farebox. All he could see, though, were a few buttons. "I'm sorry, ma'am," he said, "but all I see are some buttons." "That's right," she replied, "they are buttons. All of my friends at the home use buttons for the bus. They aren't being treated like this." The driver sighed and said, "I understand, I do. But just because others use buttons doesn't make it fare."

LIKE IF WALDO FROM "WHERE'S WALDO" WAS A CITY AND NOT A CREEPY DUDE IN STRIPES

Katie was not going to give up so easily. It had been hours now since she was challenged to find all of the world capitals on the map. She had been mostly successful so far, but the capital of South Korea was proving to be complicated. It didn't seem to matter if she zoomed in, zoomed out, or pored over every millimeter. She simply could not find it on the map anywhere. "Admit it," Gloria laughed from behind her, "you've lost. Give up." "No way," Katie quipped back, "I refuse to give…" Just then, her eye caught it, a random dot on the map that til now had eluded her. "I found it!!" she exclaimed, "I found it, finally! After hours of Seoul searching!"

FALLING EVEN FATHER BEHIND

The young man was anxious. His wife was about to have their first child, and all he could do was pace back and forth, muttering, "I'm a father... I'm a father...". Suddenly an older gentleman stopped him and said, "slow down, son. You aren't a father yet. That baby needs to pop out first." The young man paused and said, "so what you're saying is...". "Yep," the older man replied, "once that baby pops out, you're dad on arrival..."

IT'S ALL GREEK TO ME

Timmy's presentation was amazing. He brought a whole collection of short-sleeved shirts from all of the World Cup countries featuring the greats of European football - Pele, Messi, Beckham, to name a few - and a multitude of statistics about the game. When he finally sat down, exhausted, his teacher stood up and said, "wonderful presentation, Timmy, but we are currently studying ancient Greece, specifically ancient Greek philosophers, so I'm pretty sure I didn't ask for a presentation on soccer tees."

STYX TO WHAT YOU KNOW

For the science fair, I tested a theory of mine, that the Greek underworld would fold when dunked underwater. I built a scale model of the underworld, placed in a large water tank, and watched with joy as, sure enough, the model began to twist and fold. Successfully having tested my hypothesis, I invited everyone to see my immersed Hades bends.

IT'S THE GOSPEL SAWTOOTH

"And this is the Christianity wing," the museum tour guide told his group, "over here is a vial of the wine changed from water, here is the basket that held the loaves and fishes." The group was mystified as the guide carried on. "And this here," the tour guide continued as he pointed towards an old, weathered hatchet, "is the hatchet Jesus' followers used after his ascension to clear trees - the ax of the apostles."

YOU WANT IT, BABY, YOU GOT IT ...
JUST MOVE A BUST

The manager of the sculpture manufacturers was frantic. He had an enormous order to fill, 25 busts of Abraham Lincoln for the new museum, but his chief sculptor was insistent upon working on a large statue of a former Soviet leader. Finally, he had enough. "George," he called out, "we have to work on the Lincolns, so quit Stalin."

A E, I O U ONE

Billy gulped as he walked up to the microphone at the national spelling bee. He was an amazing speller, but his condition made things difficult - he hoped that his word would, at the very least, be consonant heavy. To Billy's dismay, the emcee said, "spell bookies." He sighed then started - "b - grrr,o - grrr,o - k - grrr,i - grrr,e - s." "That is correct," the emcee confirmed, "but why the grrs?" "I'm sorry, sir," Billy replied, "I suffer from irritable vowel syndrome."

LORD VADER, WE'LL FLUSH OUT THE REBELS

The construction of the new Death Star was proceeding far quicker than expected. Fearing that the Rebels may attack and destroy their latest project, Imperial engineers suggested creating an energy shield around it. Once the Emperor gave his permission, they got to work. The only feasible way they could create such a large shield was to house the energy generator on the forest moon nearby and project the force field from there to surround the Empire's newest station. The demand to do this came with the expectation of a rapid turnaround. To meet the deadline expectation, the generator and the building that housed it were constructed and operational within days. Unfortunately, this meant that washrooms were not available right away, so all Imperial staff had to use outhouses that were around the perimeter. It took a few days, but finally, they were able to install Endor plumbing.

I WOULD TOTALLY HAVE REMEMBERED THIS FROM SUNDAY SCHOOL

"Seriously, dude," Billy began to explain, "I heard it at church this morning. The pastor was reading the Bible lesson, and he flat out said it. It's gotta be true!" "No way," his friend Ralph insisted, "the Bible was written hundreds of years ago. There is absolutely no way it happened." "But listen," Billy pleaded, "it's right at the beginning of the movie – "A Long Time Ago In A Galaxy Far, Far Away." The timeline could work. And just because we only saw them in the Endor forest doesn't mean that they couldn't also have been on the oceans." Ralph was impressed – Billy wasn't so adamant very often, but he also knew that he couldn't have his friend believing something so absurd. "Okay, okay," Ralph finally replied, "I'll let you have that it could be possible. But I'm telling you, I really do think you misheard your pastor. I believe it's "He walks," not "Ewoks," on water."

I WON'T BE SHARON MY BRAM FLAKES - MY SUPPLY IS VERY LOIS

I invited Sharon over to practice her figure skating skills on my backyard ice rink. She came over but had just been at the local pub partaking in some beverages. However, her skating routine was virtually flawless- everything other than her triple axels. She asked what I thought of the routine, and I replied, "it was good, but the spin on my rink did stink, I think - skip on a drink or two."

NO MORE THAN TREE ITEMS AT A TIME

Lance was getting flustered. The self-checkout terminal was simply not working anymore. He had been able to check out half of his purchases, but now it was stuck. He called the clerk over. She took a look at the machine and then the items Lance had already scanned through. She picked up one piece, a long devotional poem to tree exteriors, and asked, "Is this yours?" "Well yes, of course it is," Lance replied. The clerk looked at it and then back at the machine and said, "that's the problem, sir - you forgot to scan this bark ode."

SUM LIKE IT HOT

"So, the total comes to…" the salesman quipped as he manually added up the bill, "$1988.89. But just a moment." The salesman then took a large, serene-looking block of metal alloy out of his pocket, rubbed the invoice on top of it, and confirmed, "yes, $1988.89." "What was that for?" the customer asked, pointing at the block. "Oh, that," he replied, "well, my math is pretty good, but I do like to run the numbers through the calm pewter first."

ABOUT TIME THEY MERMAID A DECISION

"The referees are just reviewing the feed to see if a goal was scored on the last play," the announcer said. It was a pivotal call in the hockey game, but a difficult one since the puck could not easily be seen crossing the goal line. They pored over the video, replaying over and over again, but still weren't able to agree. Finally, they looked up, and the little mermaid they had hoisted high above the ice gave a thumbs up. "It's a goal!" the announcer exclaimed, "confirmed with the Ariel view."

I'M SURE IT WILL ALL
PETER PAN OUT IN THE END

"In you go," the officer said as he threw Captain Hook in the cell, "you can call your lawyer soon." As she locked up the door, her captain walked over. "Is that who I think it is?" he asked. "Sure is, captain," she replied, "Captain Hook. He's been arrested on assault charges." "Hm," the captain pondered, "I would never have guessed. Who did he assault?" "That I don't know, sir," she replied, "beats Smee."

SHOULD HAVE STUCK WITH BEER

"How did you know?" the drug kingpin lamented as the police cuffed him. "I'll tell you," the police captain kicked in, "we knew about your great fondness for Strongbow, so we bought a limited edition 6 pack of it, placed a series of high tech bugs in the bottles and sent them to you. Once you had them out of the case, these bugs took audio and video recordings of your dealings, hacked your network... enough evidence to put you away for years. We had incider information."

WHY I OTTER...

In a highly controversial move, the Calgary Zoo was allowing corporate sponsorship of their animals — Red Rose Florist skunks, Shell turtles, Old Navy seals, Spitz swallows - and was announcing the latest at a press conference. A German food and beverage brand was taking up sponsorship of the heron exhibit. As the chief zookeeper took to the mic and the meeting began, one reporter asked, "don't you feel awful that it has come to this, or are you content with this sponsorship initiative?" The zookeeper thought a moment, shrugged his shoulder, and said, "I have Knorr egrets."

YOU HAVEN'T GOT A PRAYER. HERE. MAYBE OVER THERE, THOUGH.

"And what is your faith denomination?" the census taker asked him. "Well, Catholic, I suppose," he replied as he placed his fava beans and chianti down, "but I am part of an offshoot church which believes shoes are evil, and part of another offshoot church that wears tinfoil hats during the service." "Ah, I see," the census taker said as he wrote, "you're bi-sectual."

ITS GOTTA BE SIGMUNDAY

The psychiatrist looked at the intricate stitchwork on the quilt his patient was making, sighed, and said, "you very clearly are suffering from an Oedipal complex." "You got that from my stitching?" the patient exclaimed, "that I somehow hate my father and love my mother?" The psychiatrist walked over, showed her up close, and said, "a Freud sew..."

ON NEST, IT'S TRUE

"What is going on up there?" the carpenter asked as they worked in the basement of the grand opera house, "it sounds like a lot of chirping, tweeting and clapping." "Well," the plumber replied, "it's a big festival of singing for birds. The audience is all comprised of small birds, and the show must have just ended. We're under wren ovations."

OH DEER

"Again, I need a name," the government agent pressed. "Look, I've told you what I know," the lady said, "the family hired a large, antlered North American mammal to take care of their children. I don't have the name - it's a nanny moose..."

JUMP, JIVE, THEN YOU WHALE

The curator of the Inventors Museum was showing the tourist group around. "This is Alexander Graham Bell's first working telephone," he pointed out, "this, over here, is the original phonograph made by Edison." He then motioned the group over to a large, long, hollow cylinder. "This, however, is the most impressive artifact in our museum," he explained, "and listen to this." He pressed play on the stereo nearby, and the most beautiful music began playing. "This music was recorded underwater," he continued, "from the cylinder you see here. Philip Harmonix, an inventor, created this to allow killer whales to drink more effectively, and a byproduct of that is the music you hear now." The group gasped and began to ask, "so is this...". The curator cut in, "yes - this is the famous Phil Harmonix orca straw."

COLLECT $200 FOR PASSING GLOW

The press room was abuzz with excitement as the spokesperson for Science Canada came to the podium. A scientist there had created a means of copying the biological traits that allow fireflies to glow, and they were now seeing if those traits could be useful to humans. If they could, it would open up a world of safety possibilities for nighttime workers. "I can now take questions," the spokesperson said. One young man began with, "So how close is Science Canada to releasing something commercially?" "It will take some time," the spokesperson replied, "right now, we're just in pre-luminary testing."

MAYBE GOT MIXED UP IN TRANS-PORT

"Stop!" the nurse yelled as she burst into the operating room. The surgeon stopped immediately, and rather tersely spoke to the nurse, "what?!! I'm just about to start a sex change here!" "You're in the wrong room," she replied breathlessly, "this young man is in for a tonsillectomy. The sex change is in the next room." "Whew," the surgeon gasped as he stepped away from the patient, "that was a near Miss..."

YOU'RE BLOODY WELL RITE

Little known fact - during World War II most produced lumber and other wood product was being used to craft military items for the Allied forces. This also happened to be around the same time many Catholic churches were being constructed in North America. Due to this lack of wood, only a small number of ritual tables could be crafted and distributed. Architects were still free to complete their projects with some altar rations.

IT COULD BE WORSE –
THERE MIGHT HAVE BEEN A FACE OFF

"I'm really having trouble walking," Renee said to her doctor, "it seems like every step I take my feet wobble around." The doctor pondered momentarily before saying, "It sounds like you might have Kevinbaconitis." "What's that?" she queried. The doctor gently slapped her feet, and as they shook like jello, he said, "foot loose."

MY PRIDE AND JOY TO THE WORLD

Sara was angry. Everyone had different customs at Christmas, but she was almost universally treated appallingly for her taste in festive music. Sure, conversations always started warmly, but the moment people learned that her favorite Christmas music was from saxophonists like Kenny G and Clarence Clemons, they turned and walked away. "This is maddening," she thought to herself, "I should not be judged based on my sax yule preferences."

TALK ABOUT SPICING UP YOUR RESUME

Bob had just lost his job, and with the outstanding debt and family to care for, it couldn't have come at a worse time. "What am I going to do?" he cried out in the kitchen, preparing what would be one of many meager meals. "Drop it all, flee to Costa Rica," said a voice from the spice rack. Taken aback, Bob walked toward the rack and heard even more suggestions. "Burn the place down!" the cinnamon said. "Join a circus," offered the paprika. From the back, he heard, "Listen, Bob. Don't do anything rash. Take a couple of weeks for yourself. Brush up your resume, hit the job sites, and you'll be back at it in no time." "Whoa, Bob, that's perfect," the pepper stated, "that's some pretty sage advice right there."

IF AT FIRST YOU DON'T SUCCEED, TRAY TRAY AGAIN

Henry created the most beautiful veggie trays. All were in awe of not only the assortment but the presentation as a whole. This most recent one, however, was throwing him for a loop. It was just... off. His assistant began to suggest, "maybe if we put some shiitake...". "No, no," Henry cut in, "there's not mushroom for improvement."

NOT MUCH TO BASS AN OPINION ON

They all just left - the altos, sopranos, tenors - right in the middle of the concert. The conductor, Leopold, was shocked and just stood there in disbelief. Finally, someone walked over and said, "I think I know what's going on - here, have this Mentos." Leopold took it and said in disgust, "I most certainly will not have this!" "Trust me," the patron replied, "you take this, and your entire group will come back." Having few other options, he threw the Mentos in his mouth, and sure enough, his crew did start returning. "Thank you!" Leopold cried, "but how..." "There wasn't anything else you could do," his rescuer stated, "it was a re-choir mint."

WHAT THE DICKENS?

Manuel started slowly at first, a single booth near the Grand Canyon where travelers could choose which of his two donkeys they'd like to rent for a ride down the canyon trail. As time went on, he built more rental booths with even more burros to select. Now he had dozens of beautifully constructed depots, each with a large selection of donkeys. His venture was so popular it caught the attention of the national media, and as such, Manuel organized a press room where media could ask him questions. One young reporter queried, "Manuel, what do you think is the reason you are so successful?" Manuel pondered and replied, "well, I think it's because I've always had great ass pick stations."

YOU'LL HAVE TO USE YOUR NOODLE

It was daft, to be sure, but still, George struggled. There were two lines in the cafeteria, each one going after a bowl of chicken noodle soup. Same soup, but one line had bowls being filled by a large ladle while a large spoon filled the other. He knew there wasn't a difference, but somehow the choice of how the soup was dispensed mattered. As he stood, a lady behind him tapped on George's shoulder and said, "look, I get you are having trouble with this, but you're gonna have to make a choice - spooner or ladler."

THIS HAPPENS PERIODICALLY

It was a science fair put on by the university's science department to showcase the work of their students. Somehow, though, 10-year old Dexter managed to sneak in and set up his project in the corner. It was intricate, with lots of dials and flasks, and quite large in scale. Eventually, the judges made their way to his table and asked, "why are you here? You aren't a university student?" "I know," Dexter said excitedly, "but you will be amazed by this! I just need to add some nitrogen." He looked around, but sadly his nitrogen was nowhere to be seen. "While it does look impressive, young man," one of the judges piped up, "but you are clearly out of your element."

I COULD REALLY GO FOR SOME I STREAM

"It's crazy, I know," Bill started, "but so many people seem to know where I've been today, where I'm going..." "Let me stop you right there," Jim chimed in, "see that tv station across the street? They've been live-streaming your routes all day." "Wow," Bill said, "now I see the airer of my ways."

HOW DID THEY FIGURE IT OUT? I DINO

The latest theory on why the dinosaurs went extinct lies in Christianity, where scholars have interpreted biblical text to the point that they believe God came to earth and quickly brought those dinosaurs that believed up with Him to heaven, leaving the non-believers behind. It happened so fast, apparently, that these scholars have aptly named the event veloci-rapture.

IT CERTAINLY SHOWS POT-ENTIAL

There is a protest being held today in downtown Calgary by those that are 100% against the legalization of marijuana. These are people who felt personally attacked when the Canadian government approved legalization and want to make sure they make a very vocal, visible protest that shows they are still quite angry over it. You might say the Hemp Ire Strikes Back.

YOU SURE LANCELOT

Historians have learned that King Arthur ended up in Africa during his reign. Wanting to tour the area, he went to the marketplace to secure transportation, but this proved a frustrating venture. The donkey vendors wanted too much money per day. The rhino rental area had abysmal customer service. All of the domesticated transport lions had taken ill. Travel monkeys were too small. He had finally had enough when even the horse market was unable to provide reliable service. "By Galahad's beard," he raged, "is there no good transport available for the king of England in this ungodly desert!!??!" The owner of the horse shop walked up and gently said, "sir, I have an excellent feeling that you will be successful at the camel lot."

HOW DID I GET SADDLED WITH THIS

The two horses were in the games room, looking to play a game or two to pass the day. "How about Horse Candyland? Oh wait, that's for horses one year of age or younger. Let's see..." Silver said to his friend Pegasus. "There are Horse Snakes and Ladders," Silver posed before realizing it, too, was only for horses one year of age or younger. He refused to give up, though. "Horse Twister? Nope, same age suggestion. Horse Go Fish... nope. Horse Hungry Hungry Hippos, let's see... hm, nope." Finally, Pegasus interrupted him and said, "Silver, I give. I've had enough of your foalish games."

CAN YOU SEND ME THE LINK?

"How's my mum, doc?" Dolph asked as he stood outside the hospital room. "I wish I had better news," the doctor replied, "see, take a look." Dolph poked his head in the room and saw a large seabird atop his mum's head. "What on earth?" Dolph loudly queried. "Your mum had a major spurt of activity this morning and made a large number of German sausages," the doctor explained, "but as she began regressing, she traded those sausages for the seabird we have here." Dolph sighed and replied, "I see. She's taken a tern for the wurst."

I SAY LOCH HIM UP

"Witchcrraft, I tell ya!" Robert yelled as he pointed at MacHeath, "I've seen it! MacHeath is evil!!" "Calm down, Rroberrt," the leader of the clan said calmly, "what makes you say that?" "I walked into his worrkshop the otherr day, and therre he was, making Scottish clothing out of wood!" Robert replied. "Aye, that's not grreat," the leader said quietly, "MacHeath, what have you to say on this matterr?" MacHeath cleared his throat and replied, "it's trrue - I have been dabbling in the oak kilt."

... AND SPEAKING OF RAIN GEAR...

Stan was walking outside in the rain when suddenly the rain changed from water to what appeared to be small, rusty engine parts. He dashed inside, grabbing one piece on the way. He looked it over, found a serial number, and googled it to find that it was from the gear assembly on a 1971 240Z. Stan took out his cell, called his wife, and said, "honey, be careful out there – it's raining Datsun cogs."

ICON HARDLY BELIEVE THIS IS HAPPENING

"The weirdest thing," Bob began explaining, "ever since I updated my phone with the newest software release – whenever I touch an icon, it begins to smile and giggle." "Oh yeah, I just read about that," Jen replied, "they're releasing a fix for that, but apparently it's nothing to worry about and doesn't hurt anything – it's just an app tickle illusion."

YOU'RE DAMNED IF YOU DON'T,
YOU'RE DAMNED IF YOU MOUNTAIN DEW

The lesser demon walked into the Hell Bar and asked the barkeep, "I'm thirsty and looking for the best thing you have to drink!" "Well, I can think of a few," the barkeep replied, "Beelzebub is quite fond of this black rum here. Zuul swears by this hard lemonade, and ol' Scratch himself would tell you nothing beats a whiskey." The barkeep then walked over to the taps and said, "but I think this is what you're looking for." He poured a pint of a white liquid and brought it over. The demon took a sip and exclaimed, "Holy He who shall not be named down here... that is absolutely delicious!! What is it?" "You see that large group of demons over there?" the barkeep asked, "well, they banded together and created this, a milk unlike any other." "Wow," the demon replied, "this is amazing!" "I'm a little surprised you haven't heard of it, actually," the barkeep said, "it's Legion dairy."

THE SPIRIT OF ADIO

Matt was impressed – such a vast and varied record store, with practically every band, genre, and tangible music medium available. The only thing he found odd was that there was nothing for groups that started with the letter R. He continued to look around when from behind, he heard, "can I help you, sir?" He turned to see the staff member who had asked. "Just looking," Matt replied. "Take your time," she suggested, "no Rush."

I DON'T KNOW, BUT SUM ONE DID IT

"Okay, hotshot," the police interrogator began, "I'm going to need you to answer a few questions." It had been a horrific murder, and this was their number one suspect. The interrogator started, "5+2 equals...". "6," came the reply, and so the questioning continued. "7+7?" "12." "2+2?" "3." The interrogator paused a moment – sure, there was an alibi, but something just didn't add up.

HOPE HE'S BETTER AT LIFE CHOICES

"So, it's her, right?" Sam asked Phil. "Nope, nope – that's Beth's sister," Phil replied. "Then her, there – it has to be," Sam added. "Again, no," Phil said, "that's her cousin." "Her, there?" Sam asked again. "Sigh, no – that's her granddaughter," Phil replied exasperatedly. And it went on a few more minutes before Phil finally said, "seriously, Sam. I funeral. Beth is the one in the casket." Sam, slightly embarrassed, replied, "I'm so sorry, Phil – my vision's good, but I have terrible death perception."

THAT'S AN INTERESTING YOUR TURN OF EVENTS

Nancy sat on the bus, tears rolling down her face as she read the latest novel from her favorite author. "You alright, miss?" the driver asked. "Oh, yes – I'm sorry," she replied, "this book is just so sad, but so good." "What's it about?" he asked. "About two nurses who work together at the front desk of the emergency department, prioritizing incoming patients on need," she explained, "and they desperately love one another, but can never be together." "That is sad," he answered. "Yes, it is," Nancy said, "sad, even triagic."

THAT SMELLS RANK

Some people say that the Canadian army has an excessive number of commanding officers, but I think that's an over-generalization.

IT WILL BE GOOD TO GET BACK TO PARANORMAL

I'm no expert, but I suspect that demons hate exorcisms because their possessions are taken away.

GOING AGAINST THE GRAIN

"So how much grain seed are you carrying?" the weigh station officer asked. "About 1500 kg, sir," the trucker replied. The officer offset the scale by 1500 kg and only then recorded the weight of the truck and it's contents. "You're good to go," the officer said as he waved. "thanks, but I've gotta ask - why did you need to know about the seeds?" the trucker enquired. The officer sighed and said, "the government just passed a law that all trucks driving through Canada must have the weight of any grains offset when being weighed. It's a Canadian millet tare force."

EURO SO RIGHT, IT DOES SUCK

"I'll be down in a moment," Eunice shouted, "just vacuuming upstairs here." Almost 20 minutes went by until Eunice came downstairs, vacuum in hand, looking beyond frustrated. "What's wrong?" Hilda asked. "It's this vacuum," Eunice replied as she threw it to the floor, "it takes forever to work. It does a good job but takes way to long." "Here, let me take a look," Hilda said as she picked up the vacuum. After looking around the machine for a bit, she finally said, "ah, as I suspected. This was made in Bratislava. It's a slo-vac."

WHEN YOUR HOPS GO ASTRAY

Farmer Bill looked at the poor beast with pity. Sure, the rabbit had come and had been eating his crops for three weeks now, but when Bill found him in a cold, dark corner of the barn, he realized his nemesis was all alone. Wanting to find a better situation for the rabbit, he picked him up, drove out about an hour and stopped. Holding the bunny, he stepped out of the truck and spoke. "Listen, critter," Bill began, "over that way, there's a large habitat of rabbits. Over there is another one. If you look just over that hill, there is another large group, and finally, behind us over yonder is yet another one." Bill paused, letting the rabbit take the information in before resuming, "so you've got some choices, but under no circumstances are you to return to my farm. You've been four warrened."

ALPHABET YOU DIDN'T SEE THAT COMING

The professor, an expert in the evolution of the English language, began. "If you look up here," she said as she pointed to the top of the board, "you'll see that thousands of years ago the vowels were grouped and remain that way today. What you'll notice, though, is that over time, the other letters of the alphabet separate from one another. This is known as consonantal drift."

I READ ABOUT THIS IN THE MOOSEPAPER

It's a little-known fact that the government has conscripted a large number of does and bucks for covert espionage assignments. They are very good at it, apparently – they don't look suspicious, and they have an extensive, intricate communications system to share intel. This, of course, is known as the spy deer web.

SERBS YOU RIGHT

The theory of evolution is complete bollocks. The evidence is clear - the world was made over seven days by eastern Europeans from Zagreb. That's right - I believe in Croatianism.

I SUPPROSE ITS FOR THE BEST

Albert wasn't one to criticize, especially works of artists, but he felt that he couldn't let the latest work from the local poet laureate be published without saying something. He called Stuart in and asked him to sit down. "Stu," Albert began, "you know how much I appreciate your talent. The poems you've written in the past are just beautiful. But I have to ask - what is up with this newest one?" Stuart looked confused and replied, "what do you mean?" Albert turned his monitor around so Stuart could see. "Right here," Albert began, "this second stanza here is the same as the first stanza. Word for word, except you have it written backward. Why?" Stuart smiled and said, "oh, that! Yah - that's just a re-verse, Al."Top of FormBottom of Form

THANK GOODNESS ITS NOT A HIPPO REPLACEMENT

The vet gently stroked the majestic elephant's trunk. The elephant had been picked up and driven into Nairobi by the park wardens after they noticed it had trouble chewing. The vet looked inside the mouth of the beast, poked around a bit, and shook his head. "This isn't good," she said, "See how much her teeth are wiggling? She needs major veterinary dental work, and I can't do that here." The wardens slumped forward at the news. "Is there anything we can do?" one piped up. "There's only one place in the world that can do this for her, and it's in the southern US," the vet said, "and we can definitely get her there. But we have to move quickly." The wardens perked up, ready for action. "Alright," the vet added, prepare her for the trip to Tuscaloosa."

HOW DID IT HAPPEN?
I'M AT A FLOSS TO EXPLAIN IT

The accused took his place at the front of the courtroom. The local strip mall had been horrendously vandalized, with all of the storefronts, parked cars, and medical offices being hacked at with a hatchet, and the only person arrested so far was this one young adult. "You, young man, know that you are charged with property damage to a number of different locations. How do you plead?" the judge asked. The accused answered, "your honor, I confess that I did attack the dentist's office with a hatchet but left immediately after. I did not destroy any other part of the strip mall." The defense lawyer then stepped in. "Your honor, we do have evidence to back up this claim," she said. "Please look at the screen here," she continued as she began playing a video, "this is security camera footage from that night." As the grainy video played, the entire courtroom could see that, indeed, the young man was telling the truth. "That will do, counsel," the judge bellowed, "you only damaged the dentist office. I dismiss all other charges and sentence you to time served on the one charge. Clearly ax in dental."

ITS EXSPANSIVE TO DO EVERY DAY

"How much did they charge to cross the bridge?" Patrick asked. "$5," replied Sean, "and they wouldn't let me cross until I paid it." Patrick shook his head. "No way," he said, "there's never been a fee to go across there before." "I swear to you, $5," Sean said adamantly, "at least that's what I was tolled."

WHO SINGS THE HARMINGY?

The director didn't like what he heard. They had been rehearsing "Flu - The Musical" for days now, but the big musical number was... off. "Okay, stop," he exclaimed, "remember - this is the song where the disease confesses her love for the afflicted. I'm just not hearing it, so let's move around a bit. Dan, Jim, and Annette - you sing the blood cell tenor part. Amy - you sing the antibiotic alto lines. Kaylee, I need you to sing harmony and Linda, you are the voice of the disease. You're going to sing the malady."

SO, THINGS AREN'T LOOKING UP?

"I have never been so embarrassed in my life!!" Edna yelled as she tore open the front door, throwing her purse violently onto the floor. "What did I do?" George asked, bewildered at the venom hurled his way. Edna stopped for a moment, sighed loudly and said, in the calmest voice she could muster, "remember I told you how we were meeting up at an essential business function of mine at a high-class restaurant?" "Of course I do," George replied, "and I did exactly what you asked me to - I attached "This Way Down" and down arrow signs to my jacket, a picture of an elevator going down on my left pant leg, a picture of an airplane landing on my right leg..." "You clearly weren't listening," Edna growled, "I asked you to dress decently, NOT descent-ly."

THIS IS WHERE I DRAW THE LINE

The crayon party was in full swing. Red, blue, green - all the popular colors were there. Magenta was off in the corner, talking to purple. Yellow was dancing with orange. Suddenly a commotion was heard at the front door. "Look again," the dark brown/grey crayon said assertively. "I swear you are not on here, sir," the security guard replied, "I've looked up and down the... oh, my, I am so so sorry. Here you are, the taupe of the list."

WHAT'S WITH THE FISHBOWL IN THE MEETING ROOM?

The station manager continued leading the new hires through the television studios. "Over to the left, there is our meteorologist, Harry Caine. On your right is the News At Night set - you can see Ann Kerr preparing her notes for the broadcast." As they walked past the set and down a corridor, the manager continued. "The boardroom on your right here has our local news team, compiling events that happened in our city today into notes for the show. And in the boardroom to your left is Sally, Jim, Beth, and Colin. Sally is sleeping with Beth's husband. Jim is sleeping with Colin's wife. Beth is sleeping with Sally's husband, and Colin is sleeping with Jim's wife. It's our four in affairs department."

MUST HAVE GOT IT FROM THAT TRAMP CHEVROLET

The Dodge Caravan slowly pulled into the body shop and stopped. The mechanic walked over as the driver stepped out and asked, "what can I help you with, sir?" The driver sighed and pointed to the antenna. "See, here," he began, "the antenna is covered in... I don't even know. But it won't wash off, and the radio doesn't work as a result." The mechanic took a closer look. Sure enough, the antenna was covered in a thick, gooey liquid. "I've seen this before," she started, "do you regularly park in a car lot, surrounded by a large number of other vehicles?" The driver replied, "yes, I do. Why?" She answered, "I figured. Here, take these two tablets and drop in the fuel tank. Your vehicle has just been in contact with many cars. It has a van aerial disease."

SITTING IDOLLY BY

As Moses came down from the mount, he saw a large group of his people surrounding a large, golden idol in the shape of a bull. Some people bowed to it, some touched it, and others just stood looking at it in amazement. He called his friend over and asked, "Hey - what's going on here?" His friend replied, "Aaron made it - he wasn't sure when you'd be back. Everyone loves it." Moses, taken aback, said, "but seriously, a golden bull? Isn't that insanely bizarre and strange?" "Well," came the reply, "it's certainly awed."

MILLIONS OF SPEECHES, SPEECHES FOR ME

Usually, the used furniture shop was quiet, which made the loud scraping and crashing coming from the back all the more strange. The manager, Beth, walked towards the convention hall department, where the noise seemed to be originating. As she rounded the corner, Beth saw a man looking at their selection of platforms, eyeing each up and dragging to one side or the other. "Can I help you, sir?" she inquired. The man turned around and began, "Perhaps. The name is Mike. Mike Crowfoan. I was the lead architect on the new convention hall downtown. It's a beautiful, grand building with comfortable seating, state of the art sound and audio equipment, the works." "Yes, I've seen it from the outside," Beth interjected. Mike continued. "However, we realized far too late that the seats at the back could not see the front podium, so we need to raise it. Our full budget has already been exceeded, so I've been tasked to find a suitable, used platform. I'm just sorting these into ones I like and ones I don't." "Okay," Beth said, "so what can I do for you?" "I have to dart out, but if you could keep these separate for now, I'll be back to choose," Mike answered as he gestured towards the pile on the left, "one of these dais."

WELL, THAT'S QUITE THE PICKLE, ISN'T IT?

The reporter was almost finished with interviewing George Glass, CEO of Daring Electronics. Daring was a new company that exploded onto the scene with its innovative ideas and products, and had, within weeks, overtaken Apple's share of the marketplace. It was a fantastic story, and she was floored to be the first reporter allowed into the building to interview Mr. Glass. "I think we're almost done here, sir," she said as she turned back to her laptop, "just one more question – It's been rumored that you personally have been the only one involved in day-to-day operations, and therefore your success is solely on your efforts. Is this true?" George sat back in his chair, smiling. "That would be quite the story now, wouldn't it?" he replied, "Not true. I am the face of the company, and while it was my initial plans that started things off, I can't take full responsibility for our success. Would you like to see my team?" "Yes, yes, I really would," she replied. So together they strode down the hallway to a large boardroom. George opened the door, entered the room, and said, "gentlemen, as you were." As she too entered the room, she was taken aback. In each chair sat a large jar of pickle juice. "Um, is this a joke, sir?" she asked. George laughed. "No, no, it isn't. These jars make all business decisions, finalize product development, handle advertising," he replied, "Daring would not be successful without their guidance. They're the real brines of the operation."

Pun and Grimeish Mint

I'M NOT IMPRESSED.
PRETTY CHEESED OFF, ACTUALLY

The contractor stood at the doorway, surveying the kitchen. The owners of the home had hired him to remodel the kitchen, optimizing the area for their start-up pizza business. He made a few notes, took some measurements, and drew some rough sketches for his proposal. Stepping away from the kitchen, he met up with the couple in the living room. "Okay," he began, "I've got a few ideas here. We can reroute the sink and dishwasher to the far wall here. We can install the pizza oven right in the middle of the room. We can increase your closet space by a good 20%." The owners looked approvingly at one another. "However," he continued, "to maximize your cheese shredding space, we will have to sacrifice the microwave." The owners were startled, asking, "no microwave? Are you sure we need to get rid of that?" "Well," he replied, "it's for the grater good."

I CAN'T BELIEVE IT'S NOT BUDDHA

Constable Ted knocked forcefully on the door. A man of Arabic heritage, in his late 20s, opened the door. "Taheem Abdallah?" the officer asked. "Yes, that's me," Taheem replied, and quizzically asked, "how can I help you, officer?" Ted looked past Taheem, surveying the room. Seeming to be safe, Ted replied, "May I come in?" "Certainly, please," Taheem welcomed. Constable Ted walked in, brought out a notebook and a few photos, and began. "There was a break-in and robbery last night at the drug store, down the street here, about 10:45 pm," Ted paused before continuing, "we have a few eyewitnesses and these security cam photos that would suggest you were the perpetrator." Taheem held the photos in his hand, peered at them, and chuckled, "there's obviously a misunderstanding here, officer. That is not me. Not only does my Muslim faith speak against thievery, but I was also not in the area last night."

Ted had heard that story many times before, of course, so he sighed and said, "I'd like to believe you, but anyone I've ever arrested was "not in the area" at the time of the crime. Do you have proof?" "I do," Taheem replied, "this statue, here." Taheem pointed to a large granite carving in the living room and continued, "I beautiful sculpture, an artistic interpretation of our God, as sculpted by a talented young lady from our mosque." He reached into his pocket and pulled out a piece of paper, "I was on the other side of town at the art show at that time, purchasing this. I have the receipt here – it shows the date, time and address of the gallery where I bought the piece. I assure you, I wasn't here in the area, and that is not me." The constable looked it over. It certainly looked legitimate. He called the gallery to confirm that an art show had taken place last night and that Taheem had been one of the purchasers, and it all was on the up and up. "My apologies, Taheem," Ted said as he headed back towards the door, "we do need to follow these leads, so I appreciate your patience. Have a good night." As the door closed behind him, Constable Ted radioed into his precinct. "Hello, Sarge? It's Ted. We'll have to keep investigating. This lead went nowhere," Ted paused briefly, "the guy has a rock-solid Allah buy."

SO EASY A MONK COULD DO IT

Sal's advertised the best French fries in town, and anyone that tasted them agreed wholeheartedly with the boast. Crispy, salted just right - perfection. Jim made sure at least once a week to go in and order himself some. After several months, Jim finally dared to approach Sal, the owner, and ask, "I've gotta know, Sal - how is it your fries are the best?" Sal looked around and said, "You've been a regular customer for so long - if I show you the secret behind the fries, you can keep it quiet?" Jim could barely contain his excitement and agreed. With that, they went to the kitchen area. Nothing seemed out of the ordinary until they rounded a corner. There on the floor was a large grate covering a hole. "There," Sal said, "everything else on the menu is prepared up here, but the secret of the fries is in that hole." Jim walked over and looked down. There, a good 20 feet down, sat a Franciscan monk, chanting in Latin while using a blowtorch to prepare an order of fries. "That's the secret," Sal said, "to prepare the fries we use our deep friar."

SCRATCH THAT FROM THE RECORD

"That's the deal, mates," the record exec said. The members of Splitting Kittens looked at one another. This album was going to be their very first album released nation-wide, or at least that was the hope. What was sprung on them at the last moment was that each record had to include a sticker on the front, warning consumers about the explicit content of their songs. Fearing this would impact sales dramatically, they turned back and said, "look, we don't want to put that on the cover." The exec sighed and said, "this is the fifth time I've explained this to you, and you've declined each time. Unless you agree to this term, I can not release your record." He paused a moment to grab something from his desk drawer. It was an example of the label which read, "Parents - album contains explicit material." He stood up, shook it in front of the band members, and said, "this is your vinyl warning."

GONE GANDALFING

Bob walked by the main boardroom on his way to grab a coffee. However, something in there caught his eye, so he doubled back to take a look. At each seat, there was a long stick, about 15 in total. Bob turned to Sue, who was nearby, and asked, "what's going on in the boardroom? There are just sticks. It's weird, right?" Sue turned around to face Bob and said, "not really. The room has been booked for a while now - it's a staff meeting."

IT WAS A SPIRITED DISCUSSION

Gil, the ghost, was frustrated. The living had infiltrated his home, but he had been unable to frighten them away. He'd finally had enough and went to see the spectral psychologist. "I'm losing it, doc," he began, "I've been trying to scare these people out of my house, but it isn't working. What can I do?" "Well," the psychologist asked, "what have you been doing?" "I appear in front of them, holding my head in my hands, and shout words like "xū," "yuan" and "shěn" at them," Gil said, "but they aren't scared at all." "Ah, I see why," the psychologist stated, "it's the language you're using - you can't unease."

SO HOW DO WE AXIS IT?

The architect brought his drawings up on the screen. He had been hired by the company to design a new building, something unique and tall that would stand out over the others downtown. After a few sleepless nights, he had finally settled on this design, and this was his first chance to show it off. "So explain what you have here," the CEO asked. "Okay," the architect nervously began, "first off, it's significantly taller than the other buildings downtown, as requested, with a futuristic exterior. And it's not just a single tower, but two side by side. What sets it apart is this concept here. Tower A is perfectly straight, while tower B leans, actually is leaning towards tower A." The group looked impressed. "And there's nothing else in the world like it?" one chairperson asked. He answered, "it's unparalleled."

WHY THAT'S NO MERE CAT

The zoo administrator looked at the envelope in his hand, the bright red "Final Notice" stamp searing into his eyes. "So the subscription is over?" he asked. "We have a few days left," his aide replied. "Do we need this?" the administrator queried. He knew the answer but had hoped for something better. "That's up to you, sir," the aide said as she shuffled through the large stack of papers. "They are one of only a handful of companies that specialize in supplying zoos with African mammals, one of even fewer that accept trade-ins, and the annual subscription we have with them gives us 10% off." She then walked towards the window and continued, "and while most of our African animals are in good health, our wildebeest is in poor shape. Just look." He walked over and gazed into the wildebeest exhibit, where the old creature stumbled around and gasped heavily. "Alright then," he finally proclaimed, "we will need to re-gnu."

I'VE GOT A BEEF WITH THIS WEATHER

"To the shelter now, quickly!" Kyle yelled at the campers as he rushed them along. He knew what was coming - the clouds were telling - and if they didn't get to cover now, they would be pummeled. The last of the kids made it through the door, and Kyle slammed it shut. Suddenly it began; the din of large objects hitting the roof was deafening. One child was looking through the window and asked, "Kyle, what is happening?" "You tell me," Kyle responded, "what does it look like?" The lad looked out again and said, "it looks like... um, it looks like boat paddles falling from the sky. But they're covered in something. Is that ground beef they're covered in?" Kyle sighed, walked over, and said, "yes, yes, it is. It's a meaty oar shower."

THANKS FOR KIOSKING

As Jenny walked down the mall, she noticed a small kiosk that looked interesting, "Handbag Healer." She was in desperate need of a new handbag but so far had been unable to find one that she liked as much as her current one. She stepped closer towards the kiosk. There were fabrics, gemstones, an industrial sewing machine, and more. Jenny needed to know more, so she asked the owner, "pardon me, but what exactly do you do with handbags?" The owner, delighted to explain, replied, "We take old handbags and refurbish them in one hour or less. We repair tears, broken straps, replace material - basically make your old handbag like new again." Jenny was very intrigued but still hesitant. She held up her handbag and said, "what would you suggest for this?" The owner looked it over and said, "it isn't in great condition but only needs covering with new fabric. Leather would make an immediate difference and doesn't cost too much. Would you like me to fix this or not?" "Yes," Jenny answered, "I can be purse sueded."

I AIN'T NO HOLLAND BACK GIRL

"You will have a few daily tasks, Luuk, here at the Nederlands zoo," Thijs the zookeeper told his new assistant, "most of which are very easy, but some that must be done very carefully and precisely." Luuk pulled out his notepad and began to write as they approached the rhino exhibit. "Here," Thijs started to explain, "this is one of the tasks you must take very seriously. Rejean is our rhino, on loan from the Brooklyn zoo. Each night you must corral him into this pen, turn the key and secure this door." "That sounds easy enough," Luuk stated. Thijs sternly replied, "yes, but here is the hard part. Rejean hates Nederlandse language and will become enraged if he hears it. It is why he is in a sound-proof area during the day, but back here, there is no such safeguard. English only must be spoken in here." "Okay," Luuk said as he put his notebook away, "I think I've got it. Is there anything else?" Thijs patted the lad on the shoulder and said, "no, no. I will see you in the morning. Good night." "Goedenavond," Luuk replied. Instantly the massive beast turned hostile, stamped his feet, and began storming the gate. His howls of rage echoed through the exhibit. After a few minutes, Rejean finally calmed down again, at least enough for Thijs to corral him away safely. As he latched the door, he angrily reprimanded Luuk. "You fool!" he yelled, "you can lock, but you mustn't Dutch!"

PLEASE CLEAR THE TRI-SHARK AREA

The marine biologist took the tour group to a well-lit area of the preserve. "Over here, folks," she said, "this here is our dolphin tank. And while we love each and every one, there's a special place in our hearts for Flipper and Clipper." As she finished her opening words, two dolphins swam by, joined at the dorsal fins. "Yes, Flipper and Clipper are the only known conjoined dolphin twins in the world," she beamed. "How do you take care of them?" one child asked. "Great question," came the reply, "because of their unique nature, we are cautious about making sure each can breathe properly, keep clean, and eat. To help with that, we use this." From behind her, the biologist pulled out a large pole, the end of which had two sets of fork tines. "They must eat at the same time," she continued, which is why there are two forks. It serves a dual porpoise."

IT COULD BE A MOS-COW

The riot had finally ceased, and the prisoners were back in their cells. Irwin Penitentiary was home to the world's most nefarious, evil animals, and to see them out of their cages attacking one another had the guards on high alert. Thankfully, there was minimal damage, but there was one casualty - Penne, the mafioso monkey. Two guards, Victor and Hank, had been asked by the warden to investigate. As they looked over the body, they noticed a crude weapon sticking out of Penne's back. "Look here," Hank pointed out to his partner, "this was made out of a piece of wood, sharpened to a deadly point." Hank pulled it out of the corpse, looked it over, and said, "I know who did it." Victor was taken aback at how quickly Hank had figured it out and asked, "how?" "See how it's shaved down?" Hank began explaining, "that's done by hoof. There are cow hairs on it, so one of them did it. Finally, there's a hammer and sickle etched on it. This was the work of the Mad Bovine, Ivan the Terrible. It's a bull shiv, Vic."

WAVE YOUR HANDS IN THE AIR LIKE YOU'RE FILLED WITH... AIR...

The retiring park warden was walking the recruit around the cabin. "Thirty years I spent up here," he reminisced, "I'll miss this place. It's yours now, son, so let me explain a few things. There are dishes and cutlery over here. The forest fire lookout point is up this ladder. From the mountaintop here you can watch miles for any sign of danger. It's a beautiful view, too, but not without its challenges." They walked towards the office, and the warden continued. "Cell service is practically non-existent," he said, "the landline is good but prone to cutting out. As a result, the internet is spotty as well." The recruit then asked, "so what happens if I need anything?" "Glad you asked," the warden replied, "in this closet, we have a solar-powered wacky wave inflatable tube guy. If everything has cut out and you need something, just bring it outside, turn it on, and the bright waving will alert the base, and they'll send someone up right away." "So what we have here," the recruit began." "Correct," the warden interrupted, "what we have here is a flailer to communicate."

GOOD THINKING - I'VE GOTTA HAND IT TO YA

"Aaarrrggghhhh!!!" came the cry from the kitchen. Jan rushed in to see her daughter Cindy grasping her hand in pain, tears streaming down her eyes. "Oh no, what happened?" Jan asked. "I was walking by the stove," Cindy grimaced, "I tripped, put my hand out, and it landed on the burner!" "Let me see," Jan asked as she reached for Cindy's hand. She looked it over and said, "you're lucky - it could have been worse. It should heal up in a few days." "But mom," Cindy tearfully said, "I've got a photoshoot this afternoon for my hand modeling contract. If I don't do it, they'll drop me!" Jan pondered. It was quite the predicament. Suddenly she blurted out, "oh, yes! I know what to do!" She left the room, stormed upstairs and came back down with what looked like a jar of jelly. "This," Jan smiled as she twisted the top open, "this is your great-grandmother's concoction. It's a healing lotion - there's aloe vera, ground Asprin, sage, and several other mystery ingredients. Here." Jan took a dollop of the lotion and gently rubbed it on Cindy's burn. "That feels so much better," Cindy said, "so soothing. And... and the burns are fading away!" "Yes, it's a miracle," Jan glowed, "problem salved."

LIKE A SPRING SENTENCE, BUT WARMER

Hal stood at the bus stop, shivering as the snow cascaded down. He was thankful to have the job, but his wages only covered the essentials of life. Hal's old denim jacket was all he had for cover. A parka was simply not affordable, so all he could do was hope the bus came soon. Just then, a Mercedes drove by and pulled over. An older man stepped out, approached Hal, and said, "you look bitterly cold. Here." The man reached into his pocket, pulled out a piece of paper, and pinned it on Hal. Almost instantly, Hal started warming up. "Thank you so much," Hal exclaimed, "but I have to know - what is going on?" "Read it," the man said as he walked away. As the man drove off, Hal looked down at the piece of paper. On it was written, "Winter is on my head, but eternal spring is in my heart." Hal then knew what a precious gift he had been given - a winter quote.

CAN ONE MURDER A MURDER?

Two large black crows sat in the courtroom, awaiting their turn with the divorce judge. Finally, their time came, and the judge began. "Just looking over your petition for divorce, Mrs. Crow," the judge said as he shuffled through the court papers, "and I don't know that you have enough to warrant this action. Can you tell me, in your own words, exactly why I should grant you this divorce?" Mrs. Crow hopped up on the desk and began squawking, as a crow does, at the judge. The judge took it all in, taking in each shrill call. When she was done, the judge turned to the court recorder and said, "I stand corrected. Begin divorce proceedings immediately." The recorder looked back at the transcript and asked the judge, "um, okay, but on what grounds? I couldn't understand her - it just sounded like normal crow chatter." The judge replied, "is it not obvious? Divorce has been granted on the grounds of just caws."

THAT'S TWO CRAPPY

It was an odd relationship, but beautiful at the same time. Suzette, the bearded lady, had found true love with the newest member of the sideshow - Two Buttocks Billy, the man with two bums. As they sat together after the show, they shared a root beer and gazed into each other's eyes. "Oh, Billy, I have never been so happy," Suzette sighed. "Nor I, Suzette," Billy lovingly said back, "and you are so beautiful. Why I think you'd win any beauty pageant out there!" Suzette blushed. "That's so sweet, Billy," Suzette said, "but you know that isn't true." "It is! It is so very true, my love - no one is as lovely as you," Billy crowed, "but I admit to being bi-assed."

THE GRILL OF MY DREAMS

"I am so sorry, sir," the waiter apologized, "but we had a mishap in the back, and your order ended up more well-done than normal." "Oh, okay, but what happened?" the man asked. "There was a small fire," the waiter answered, "and your meal got, well, singed." "That's okay," the man said, "I actually prefer my food very well done. I'll just have it." "Very well," the waiter said as he walked away. Moments later, he came back with the plate, and as requested, each portion was blackened. "Looks good!" the man stated, "but help me out a little. That's the steak, there's my potato, carrots... but this portion here - it doesn't look recognizable." "That, sir, is your salad," the waiter said. "Ah, okay," the man said as he poked at it, "what kind?" "Leafy green salad," the waiter replied, "mostly chard."

AT LEAST SHE WASN'T DEFEETED

"Quickly, please!" Dan shouted as he burst into the Sumatran hospital, "my friend - she's shattered her foot!" A nurse ran to the door and took Liza to the back. Visibly shaken, Dan stumbled to a chair and sat. After a few minutes, a doctor came out and handed Dan a coffee. "It's alright, son," the doctor said comfortingly, "she's on painkillers right now and sleeping." "Thank you," Dan replied, grateful for the coffee and the company. A nurse walked by and handed the doctor an envelope containing X-rays. The doctor looked them over and said to Dan, "if you're ready, we can discuss what is going on with your friend." Dan nodded so he continued. "The bones in her right foot have been shattered. In fact, the digits here have broken into dozens of pieces. What happened?" Dan replied, "we were hiking up a dormant volcano when she screamed and fell to the ground. I didn't see what caused it. I just knew her foot was horribly injured." "Where were you hiking?" the doctor asked. Dan answered, "Krakatoa."

I REALLY TAIWANED ON LAST NIGHT...

"Man, that new hire is something," Jeff said to Andy, "he's already pushing for things to get done, he's ambitious, impatient and holy crap is he ever competitive." "Yeah, I've heard," Andy replied, "but it's not all that surprising. You know where he comes from, don't you?" Jeff shook his head, so Andy continued. "He came to the country from Taiwan," Andy explained, "he's just got a Taipei personality."

MAYBE HE COULD TEAM UP WITH PRIVATE AMERICA AND APPLIANCE MAN

Fun fact - did you know that the original concept for the Marvel hero "Doctor Strange" called for him to be a police officer, not a doctor? The basic idea was still the same - debilitating injury forces Strange to look to the world of magic. However, despite the overt enthusiasm displayed by most of the company, Stan Lee was much less cop-to-mystic.

WAY TO STATE THE OBVIOUS

The two scientists stared at the object before them. It was a strange, strange discovery. It existed as a gas, liquid, and solid simultaneously, and as one phase would change, the others would as well, so it was in this constant state of flux. "I have never seen anything like it," the younger scientist finally said, "what about you?" The other scientist looked it over and replied, "no, no. Never. I have never seen or heard of an object that exists in all three states at once." "What should we call it?" the young scientist asked. "Whatever," her cohort answered, "it doesn't matter."

I'M FEELING BRAZILL

Carlos could not find what he was looking for. His new girlfriend Dee was sitting on the couch, passion in her eyes, but he couldn't get in the mood. He kept flipping through all the radio stations - pop didn't help, country certainly didn't, hard rock didn't either. "Just come over here, Carlos," Dee begged. "My love, I can't," he replied, "I need to find a song that will help me treat you like a queen." Finally, he came across a station that played Brazilian music. Overjoyed, he leaped over the couch and began kissing Dee. "Oh, my," Dee gasped, "why does this music get you in the mood?" "Because," Carlos replied, "I need samba, Dee, to love."

IT'LL GET THROWN ABOUT IN COURT

"Admit it! You did it!" The constable barked as he interrogated Sally. "I swear it wasn't me," Sally calmly replied, "I have an alibi and everything." The constable sat in his chair, fuming. Someone committed the crime, and Sally was the only suspect, but she wasn't moving from her story. They were still in the process of confirming her alibi, but the early talk was that it was legitimate. As far as crimes go, it wasn't heinous. Nevertheless, the culprit had entered various homes and threw paperwork all over the main floor. Sally sat smugly, knowing they had nothing on her, and expecting release within the hour. Just then, a knock on the door came, and the constable was asked to come out. A few minutes passed when the constable came back into the room, a file folder in hand. "Alright, Sally," he grinned, "one last chance. I have video surveillance footage from one of the homes that shows someone who looks verrrrry similar to you throwing trash and paper all over the place. Are you, Sally Messier, the one that has been littering homes with thrown about items?" Sally cried and confessed, "yes, it's me. It's strew."

I SEA WHAT YOU DID THERE

Plaidbeard, the fearsome Scottish pirate, was notoriously negative about, well, everything. He very rarely agreed with anything his crew suggested, and even when he did, it was because that's what his intentions already were. His rote answer to any question was invariably, "nae, you scallywag!" No one on his crew was free from his negativity, save the lady, Guinevere. He had hired her on to his crew just last year, a lass just as tough and foul-mouthed as any other pirate. She worked her way up to be one of Plaidbeard's most trusted crewmen. Guinevere was also the only one to be talked to positively by Plaidbeard. No matter how outlandish her questions, requests, or suggestions were, the old sea dog immediately agreed. This didn't go unnoticed by Guinevere, and while she was glad Plaidbeard was agreeable with her she was concerned about the feelings of the other crew towards her. So she pulled Plaidbeard aside one day and asked, "Captain, why do you always say yes to me but always no to anyone else?" Plaidbeard leaned in and said, "listen, lassie - those scallywags only deserve naes. But you - I only have ayes for you."

THEY'RE COMING TO TAKE ME A-WAIL

The court administrator was almost done splitting out today's cases between the three judges on duty. "We have a vandalism charge here – you can take that one, Jim," she said as she dropped the file folder on the third of three piles, "that now leaves just one more case for trial today." She opened up the last file to look over the details and said, "okay – this one's different for sure. Reg Fenton, arrested for excessively weeping and crying in public. The arresting officer writes that Mr. Fenton's wailing in public exceeded noise bylaws and caused a great deal of disturbance. Who wants to take it?" The three judges looked at each other, hoping one of the others would volunteer for the case. After minutes of silence, the three still could not decide who should take it. Finally, the administrator huffed in frustration and said curtly, "fine, I guess it's yours, Linda. The bawl's in your court."

DEER MR. DISNEY

I learned an interesting fact today about Walt Disney. When scoping out the classic film "Bambi," his financial backers at the time were not pleased with the project. Their main concern was the scene where Bambi's mother is shot and killed. They felt that keeping it in the movie would severely impact their returns. Walt, however, was adamant that the scene remain in the film, and eventually, his artistic vision won out. When "Bambi" hit theatres, it was a success. What was clearly evident, though, is that the financiers were right – it would easily have doubled or even tripled the return on investment. This means that they lost a lot of doe on the film.

I'VE GOTTA HAND IT TO YOU...
AND HEAD, FOOT TO YOU FOR FREE

The young lady strutted into the bank, fully poised and with a palpable air of confidence about her. As she walked over to the teller, she pulled out a large stash of money from her purse, laying it all out on the counter when she came to the window. "I'll need this counted and deposited directly into my account," she demanded sweetly. The teller began sorting out and tallying the cash before him. After a few minutes, he was done and said, "that's $50,000, ma'am." He held it in his hand and placed it in a security bag and asked, "I don't mean to pry, but may I ask where this money came from?" The young lady smiled, leaned in, and answered, "well, it's not necessarily legal, but it's not NOT legal. I sell black market Barbie parts. Not heads or legs, though. I'm a small arms dealer."

WELL I HAD A BEEF TO SETTLE

Joe, the lead cowboy, his face frozen in bewilderment, looked at the field before him and shook his head. Jed brought his horse up alongside and asked, "what's up, Joe?" Joe sat silent for a bit before responding. "It's the damndest thing, Jed," Joe managed to whisper, "not two minutes ago I had grouped all the cattle just over here. And now... look there, there. They ain't together. The whole group has scattered all over. It's impossible, ain't it?" Jed sighed and said, "it's not un-herd of."

SOMETHING TO GRAVE ABOUT

The chief coroner sighed. He hated this part of the job, but it had to be done. The aircraft had crashed shortly after taking off. While a miraculously large amount of passengers were able to walk away with only minor injuries, the ones towards the end of the vessel weren't quite so lucky. So he held the passenger list in his hand and walked through the smoldering wreckage. It helped somewhat, but he knew that he would need help in identifying most. He called out to his team and asked them to come in. "Alright, team," he began, "I've done a run-through and identified some of the bodies, but from this whole area over here we need to remove who and what we can gently." He retook a look and continued. "I've already sorted into two piles – ones that we will need DNA testing done for identification and ones that we should be able to identify visually." "Pardon, sir," a team member asked from behind, "which is which?" "Fair enough," he replied, "It's been a long night for me. I think that's the pile we'll need help for there." He pointed to an area to his left, but hesitated. "… or over there. But that over there," he said definitively, "that's remains to be seen."

HELLO, I'M YOUR CAMP PAIN MANAGER

The discussion, to put it mildly, could be heard throughout the Elkentrout Camping and Hunting shop. "Sir, please, I assure you that this tent is 100% Canadian made," the sales associate said. "That's bollocks, and you know it!" the angry customer shouted, "if this is Canadian made, then paint my butt cheeks purple and call 'em the Wonder Twins!" "Sir, I don't know what to tell you," the associate said in exasperation, "in our catalog here it says that this model is made here. May I ask why you're certain it's NOT made in Canada?" The customer gave a half-smile and began. "The canvas is a material that is only found in China. The zipper configuration is unique to the southwest region of China. The instructions are in broken English. And, lastly," he asserted, "there's a little tag on the inside, just above the door, that says "Made in China." The associate sighed and said, "I just don't know what you want from me. I'm just telling you what it says in our catalog. What does it matter, anyway? It's solid, completely weather-proof, a reasonable price-point...". "Because," the customer interrupted, "it's import tent."

YOU DON'T NEED TO BE SUCH A BEACH ABOUT IT

"Cut!" The director yelled for the fifth time that hour. Sure, "Surfer Navy" was never going to win an Oscar, but he still had a vision for it, and the lead actor was just not getting it. "Gavin, can I see you over here, please," the director asked the star. He motioned towards a table, and both men sat across from one another. "Gavin, I love the work you're doing, I really do," the director began, "but I've gotta be honest with you. You're enunciating every syllable like you're on a stage performing for the Queen of England. There's more ham in your performance than at the local Subway shop." Gavin looked puzzled at first, then replied, "but I'm playing the captain of the submarine. It needs gravitas." "Yes, you're the captain," the director returned, "but you are a former surfing champion, one who lives the beach life even in this position of authority. It's a comedy, for crying out loud, not Saving Private Ryan. You need to take the performance down a notch, throw more "gnarly," "sweet," and "righteous" into your lines." Gavin was about to argue, but the director was insistent. "Chill, have fun with the role," he said, "I need you to be more sub dude."

FIN

Printed in Canada